MW00424748

Praise for *Coach to Coach*

"For great performances in your profession and family ... study this book!"

Dan Gable
Olympic gold medalist, three-time U.S. Olympic team coach
15 NCAA team titles, University of Iowa Wrestling
355-21-5 lifetime coaching record

"Some books you read for entertainment. Some you read for enlightenment. *Coach to Coach* will give you both."

Coach Lou Holtz
1988 NCAA National Champions, Notre Dame Football
Only coach to lead six different college programs to bowl games
College Football Hall of Fame

"*Coach to Coach* is an important reminder of the power of a coach. If you want to help more people and make a positive impact on the lives of others, read this book!"

Jon Gordon
Best-selling author of The Energy Bus, The Carpenter, *and* Training Camp

"*Coach to Coach* is about human development through sports. Martin Rooney gets it EXACTLY right in very clear ways: Elite coaching is about relationships, character development, and accountability."

Anson Dorrance
22 NCAA Championships, University of North Carolina Women's Soccer
1991 U.S. Women's Soccer World Cup Champions
7-time NCAA Women's Soccer Coach of the Year and 1987 NCAA Men's Coach of the Year
U.S. National Soccer Hall of Fame

"Finding the right coach at the right time had an incredible impact on my life. In today's sports and business world, there has never been a more important time to have responsible and ethical people in place serving as coaches. *Coach to Coach* offers you practical and user-friendly tips on how best to be THAT coach for someone else."

Shawn Johnson
Olympic gold and silver medalist in gymnastics
Winner of ABC's Dancing with the Stars

"*Coach to Coach* tackles the challenges and joys that come from a life of coaching. Use these simple coaching strategies and you will have no choice but to help more people."

Phillip Fulmer
1998 National Champions, University of Tennessee Football
College Football Hall of Fame

"*Coach to Coach* is a must-read for anyone interested in being the best version of themselves as a coach, teacher, spouse, or parent. Martin Rooney combines wonderful teaching points with an engaging story. I have read many books on leadership and feel *Coach to Coach* will be a classic for coaches from youth sports all the way up to the professional level."

Mark Krikorian
Head coach, Florida State Women's Soccer
2014 and 2018 NCAA National Champions

"Coaching is so much more than teaching someone how to play a sport. Coaching is about teaching them how to become great at life. What they learn on the field is what they do off the field. Coach from the heart with an open mind and find value in every player … form a synergy and watch the magic happen. *Coach to Coach* is your guidebook on how to help inspire someone to live out the story of their dreams."

Rudy Ruettiger
The inspiration for the blockbuster film Rudy

"*Coach to Coach* is a great reminder of the simple coaching principles that produce results. Whether you are working with athletes on the deck at the Olympic Games or teaching young group swimmers foundational mechanics, coaches, mentors, and teachers need to practice the ideas in this book in order to offer our best coaching to the young people we are blessed to get to coach."

David Marsh
12 NCAA team titles, Auburn University Swimming
Head coach, 2016 U.S. Olympic Women's Swim Team
Coach of 54 Olympians from 21 different countries

"*Coach to Coach* is a much-needed guide that will teach you how to inspire others. Martin trained me to be my best at the NFL Combine and has now made his coaching strategies into a simple philosophy for anyone. This captivating sports story will teach you how to be a better coach no matter who it is you lead."

Chris Long
2018 Walter Payton NFL Man of the Year
Two-time Super Bowl champion

"Martin Rooney jukes right and then breaks left with *Coach to Coach*, and he scores again! As a coach, you are better after reading it. That's really all there is to it. This should be mandatory reading for all coaches at every level to learn to connect and contribute. Thank you for making me better, Martin."

Gunnar Peterson
Head strength and conditioning coach, Los Angeles Lakers

"Coaching is about doing everything in your power to bring out the best in someone else. Even the greatest coaches in the world need guidance at certain points in their careers. In his book *Coach to Coach*, Martin Rooney offers that guidance in a powerful story. With so many great relatable lessons in every chapter, this little book will help you be that coach your athletes will always remember for the right reasons."

Liane Blyn
Head of Sports Performance, Arizona State University
Multiple-time World Champion and World Record Holder in
powerlifting

"As a fighter, you rely heavily on your coaches for support and direction. Martin was always my coach, and he was able to help me by saying the right thing at the right time. Using the story in *Coach to Coach*, he masterfully teaches you how to better connect and communicate to help someone fight their next battle."

Jim Miller
First fighter to reach 30 fights in UFC history
Most career fights in the Octagon in UFC history

"After 33 years of coaching, I have learned there is a lot more than the X's and O's of the game. It is also about who those X's and O's are and how you can grow them as both players and people. Having watched Martin coach for years, I know he always did both. *Coach to Coach* is a valuable resource that should be on every coach's bookshelf."

Greg Toal
2009 and 2011 U.S. High School National Champions, Don Bosco
Football
Lifetime 305-55-2 coaching record

"To be a successful coach you must be likable, believable, and an example for all on your team. In each of these elements, as a coach and a leader, Martin Rooney has set the standard. If you enjoy inspiring stories with memorable characters that teach you simple wisdom, this book is for you. I highly recommend this book for anyone who considers him- or herself a coach."

Jeffrey Gitomer
Best-selling author of YES Attitude *and* The Little Red
Book of Selling

"There's more to coaching than the strategic, technical, and tactical aspects of a certain situation. Coaching also includes mentorship, leadership, and character development. A great coach instills the intangibles of discipline, resiliency, and fortitude to challenge individuals to be better than the day before. *Coach to Coach* can help you to make that connection."

Joe Kenn
Head strength coach, Carolina Panthers
2015 NFL Strength Coach of the Year

"*Coach to Coach* provides an easily relatable view into the frustrating but equally exhilarating profession of coaching. This is a book I would recommend to anyone looking to improve as a coach, regardless of sport."

Tony Veney
Head coach, track and field and cross country, Ventura College
2017 USA Track and Field Coach/Educator of the Year

"For every coach who spends all their time investing in others, but feels like no one has time to invest in them, Martin Rooney hears you, and *Coach to Coach* is lesson number one."

Nick Winkelman, PhD
Head of Athletic Performance and Science for Irish Rugby Football Union

"*Coach to Coach* was my reminder of why I wanted to coach. Every athlete will leave sports someday and need skills for real life. This book inspires coaches to be positive role models and do our job to instill these skills. Read this book and you will help more people succeed."

Shauna Rohbock
Olympic silver medalist in bobsled
Assistant coach, U.S. National Bobsled Team
President's Council on Sports, Fitness, & Nutrition

COACH

to

COACH

MARTIN ROONEY

AUTHOR OF *TRAINING FOR WARRIORS*

COACH
to
COACH

AN EMPOWERING STORY ABOUT
HOW TO BE A GREAT LEADER

WILEY

Published by John Wiley & Sons, Inc., Hoboken, New Jersey.
Published simultaneously in Canada.

For general information on our other products and services or for technical support, please contact our Customer Care Department within the United States at (800) 762-2974, outside the United States at (317) 572-3993 or fax (317) 572-4002.

Wiley publishes in a variety of print and electronic formats and by print-on-demand. Some material included with standard print versions of this book may not be included in e-books or in print-on-demand. If this book refers to media such as a CD or DVD that is not included in the version you purchased, you may download this material at http://booksupport.wiley.com. For more information about Wiley products, visit www.wiley.com.

Library of Congress Cataloging-in-Publication Data:

Names: Rooney, Martin, 1971- author.
Title: Coach to coach : an empowering story about how to be a great leader / Martin Rooney, Author of Training For Warriors.
Description: Hoboken, New Jersey : Wiley, [2020]
Identifiers: LCCN 2019047743 (print) I LCCN 2019047744 (ebook) I ISBN 9781119662198 (hardback) I ISBN 9781119662211 (adobe pdf) I ISBN 9781119662204 (epub)
Subjects: LCSH: Coaching (Athletics)
Classification: LCC GV711 .R66 2020 (print) I LCC GV711 (ebook) I DDC 796.07/7—dc23
LC record available at https://lccn.loc.gov/2019047743
LC ebook record available at https://lccn.loc.gov/2019047744

Cover Design: Wiley
Cover Images: Whistles: © LuisPortugal/Getty Images, © _laurent/Getty Images

Printed in the United States of America

F10017208_012820

To my old coach Bill Scarola, who taught me you must first be on fire before you can make someone else burn.

"Our chief want is someone who will inspire us to be what we know we could be."

—*Ralph Waldo Emerson*

~~~~~

"If I accept you as you are, I will make you worse; however, if I treat you as though you are what you are capable of becoming, I help you become that."

—*Johann Wolfgang von Goethe*

Contents

Foreword

In this book, Martin Rooney is going to try to convince you that coaches have the most important job in the world. And although this sounds like a bold statement, I believe it to be true.

But I'm going to take that idea one step further.

If I were to ask you, "Who is the most important coach in the world?" you might name world leaders, powerful heads of business, or top coaches of sport organizations. You might mention an influential coach you've had in your own life, such as a special teacher or mentor, who has been the greatest help to you.

While I agree all of those people are incredibly important, I have a more personal answer. Now that I've transitioned from being a professional athlete to a coach, I realize the most important coach in the world is the person who coaches our children. And that realization is why I stand so strongly behind the message and mission of this book.

I have known and trained alongside Martin Rooney for 20 years. In many fitness and training circles, he is known as "the man" because of his technical knowledge. But that knowledge was only part of the reason I entrusted him to coach my kids. The other part was because he was able to get them to apply that knowledge through his ability to connect as a coach. During those years he spent coaching my boys, I witnessed the same strategies that Martin features in his book and I know they work.

If you are looking for simple and effective principles about how to be a great coach, they are here waiting for you in this book. But it goes beyond sports. I believe this inspirational book can also make you a better person, and someone who can make others better. Although both my sons were lucky enough to go on to play in the NFL, they learned lessons from Martin that could be used beyond the playing field. His coaching style taught them valuable lessons for winning in the game of life, too.

Whether you consider yourself a coach or not, you will be able to use the information in this quick and easy read to help people. If I could coach you how to use this book, I would challenge you to immediately apply the lessons while they are fresh in your mind, because as *Coach to Coach* will remind you, it isn't enough to know the lessons, you also need to put them into action.

It is my hope that every coach around the world reads this book. And you should hope so, too. Because not only might one of those coaches be in charge of your country, but one of them might also be a very influential part of your child's future.

Phil Simms
Super Bowl XXI MVP
Inside the NFL analyst
CBS lead sportscaster

Introduction

The world needs better coaches.

Whether you believe it or not, you are a coach. You don't have to be in charge of a sports team or business to earn the title. If you are a parent, teammate, co-worker, or friend, you are a coach in some way to someone else every day.

Unfortunately, like money, marriage, and parenting, coaching someone else doesn't come with a rule book or manual. It is my hope that this short, yet powerful parable in some way becomes one of those manuals for you.

I believe being called a coach is the most honorable title you can earn. When someone calls you "coach," he or she is handing you the reins to some aspect of their life. They give you control, hoping you are the one who cares enough to show them the way to where it is they want to go.

This book is not about current science or the technical knowledge about running a practice or helping someone win a game. The ideas are much simpler, but also run much deeper. This is the softer side of coaching we know exists, but rarely gets a glimpse in today's arena.

I believe we are all waiting for a person like the old coach in this book to show up and help us fix a number of the problems in our lives. My hope is that after reading this book, instead of continually waiting for that person to magically appear, you go out into the world, use the lessons he had to teach, and become that coach for someone else.

I promise if you just take away the "Golden Rule" from this book and apply it, your life and the lives of others around you will improve. And that is because the real way a coach becomes richer is by enriching the life of someone else.

I also invite you to share your own inspiring coaching stories or how you have used some of the ideas from this book to improve the life of someone else. You can reach me at Martin@CoachingGreatness.com.

How do I know applying what you read in this book can forever change your life? Because it worked for me.

Martin Rooney
Cornelius, NC
2020

1

The Tunnel

AND THEN HE WAS THERE.

Things really couldn't get much worse. Another loss for the team, and as Brian Knight made his way toward the locker room, he realized he couldn't be more alone.

As he walked from the field into the tunnel, he thought about slipping out a side door and going home. Not only did he really not feel like facing the team or the other coaches, but he also felt his job was in jeopardy.

But if he snuck back to his house, things wouldn't really be better there anyway, he thought gloomily. His kids would already be asleep—a reminder of another day missed with them. And quietly slipping into bed next to his sleeping wife would only remind him of the growing distance between them.

Bills and stress were piling up. Maybe it was time to give up on coaching and get a "real" job.

"Not your best day, huh, Bri?" came a hoarse voice from what seemed out of nowhere.

Brian turned around to see an older man about his height, maybe in his mid-60s, standing with his arms and palms against the cool wall of the tunnel.

"Excuse me?" said Brian, in the kind of tone that let the man know he was offended.

"I said, it didn't seem to be your best day out there," replied the old man. "It's pretty obvious the defense was the reason the team lost out there tonight. Not much to be proud of."

This got Brian's attention and angered him. Now agitated and arms crossed against his chest, he retorted, "Look, man, I don't know who you are or how you got in

here, but you picked the wrong guy to piss off tonight."
With that statement, Brian took a half-step closer to
the man.

The old man, seemingly amused by his apparent
aggression, stepped away from the wall, kept his hands at
his sides and moved right within a foot of Brian. "Calm
down, kid. Seems things are worse than I remembered.
I'm not here to bring you down. I'm here to build you
up." And with a smile that seemed to disarm Brian a little,
he added, "And besides, I really don't think you want to
lose twice tonight."

Looking into the old man's eyes, Brian saw a confidence and peace of mind that intrigued him. He could
also feel something else. It wasn't aggression. The closest
thing he could equate it to was compassion. The old man
understood. This feeling and the smile on the old man's
face actually made Brian crack a smile, too.

With the tension eased a little, the old man said,
"Don't worry, kid, everything has a strange way of
working out."

At that moment, the locker room door burst open
and the head coach yelled out, "Knight, get in here. We're
about to address the team."

Brian turned back to offer a quick apology to the
old man, but he was gone. Brian paused, puzzled about
where this man had come from and how he knew his
name. But before he could process the exchange or his
sudden disappearance, he heard his name yelled again
and quickly headed back to the locker room for the usual
postgame duties.

The rest of the night was the usual except for one thing. Yes, there was the review of the game, the plans for next week, and the long drive home. But instead of going to sleep feeling helpless, for the first time in as long has he could remember, Brian had a strange feeling of optimism that things could indeed work out just like the old man said.

2

The Grind

Every day was starting to seem like wash, rinse, and repeat. And not on a good cycle.

Getting up early for so many years had become natural to Brian, but that didn't mean it was easy. In fact, the morning knot he had in his stomach was getting tighter and putting his feet on the floor at 4 a.m. was getting tougher. More and more days started with him wishing he could just stay in bed.

Brian's two girls were also getting older and beginning to notice when he wasn't around. By the time he got home at night, they were either asleep or he was too wiped out or stressed out to do much with them. Sure, like most dads, he made it to the occasional lunch at home or school recital, but his conscience told him it wasn't enough. And when his oldest offered him some play money to buy an hour of his time the other day to stay home a little longer with her, it really hurt.

Things with his wife, Kelly, weren't good, either. She had always been on board with his dream of big-time college coaching, but the two different moves and his ever-increasing hours were taking their toll. With Kelly caring for the girls and also working as a graphic designer, conversations usually focused on their busy schedules. She had become distant and often appeared both frustrated and less interested in his dream. The most obvious proof of this disengagement was that it had been over a full season since she had attended a game to support him. "For better or for worse" seemed to Brian to be just things people unconsciously agreed to during their wedding vows. And when "the worse" started happening, it seemed like Kelly didn't remember that part of her vows at all.

Brian still loved football. Sports had always been the driver of his life. After his athletic career as a college linebacker ended, he naturally made the transition to coaching. Now almost a decade into this career path, however, he felt unprepared. And this lack of confidence became a vicious cycle of negativity and a lack of effort. He knew deep down if he kept this act up, his job wouldn't be safe for long.

On the field was where Brian always excelled. When he made the transition from athlete to coaching at his alma mater, he was familiar with the athletes he had played with and had their respect as a former star player and a teammate. This allowed him to work on the players' weaknesses and improve the defense. This led to some recognition and his and Kelly's first move up the ladder to a bigger program.

Success can often breed success, even if the success isn't yours. During his second coaching stint, Brian's team eventually won the conference championship and narrowly missed a national title. Although he didn't have the same impact on the players, the athletes on this team competed at a much higher level. Their success and a couple of first-round draft picks later, Brian appeared to be a premier coach who forged athletes at the highest level. This made him more marketable and in demand.

It was the second move and his current situation where things started to unravel. Or you could say that the truth about Brian's true coaching ability came out. Brian joined the staff of a high profile and nationally known head coach charged with rebuilding a former top program. It was going to be a tough task. The athletes wouldn't be the same caliber as those he'd coached in the past, but Brian was up for the challenge (and the increased pay and prestige, too).

The problems started for Brian when the athletes he coached didn't seem to be on board with his plan. Now ten years removed as a player (and two kids and a number of pounds heavier), Brian lacked both the command of respect and the ability to connect with the current players under his watch. The same thing was happening at home with his family, too. Of course, being a defensive-minded person, he rationalized his lack of appreciation from the team and at home as "their loss." The trouble was, according to the head coach and Kelly, if Brian didn't fix the problem and turn this season around, the loss could be his.

3

The Showup Showdown

After a game, it is usual for the team to practice the next day. Since the season is short and condensed, athletes and coaches have to maximize the time to get physically and technically ready for the next week.

After a losing game, however, morale is usually low and aggressions can run high. Practice can often seem like a softer word for punishment. On that Sunday morning after the game, Brian would find out he wasn't the only one who was in a defensive mood.

Marcus Chase was the most talented player on the defense. A top recruit out of high school from Florida, some people questioned his decision to go to a program that was rebuilding. Now in his third year with the school, even he might agree it had been the wrong choice. Not only had the team not cracked into the Top 25, but his play had been highly criticized. Just like Brian, no one likes to admit when they aren't living up to their potential.

Marcus also hadn't recovered from the fallout of the game last night. Rarely do defensive players make highlight reels on ESPN. That is, unless they end up making an offensive player look really good. During the fourth quarter, on a big third-down play, Marcus was hurdled by a receiver as he attempted to make a tackle. Not only did this acrobatic play lead to Marcus making his first Sports Center highlight, it also led to the touchdown that sealed his team's loss.

Marcus was a bit of a lone wolf on the team. His teammates also knew his football pedigree and got the feeling from Marcus that he thought he was better than they were. Marcus always put in the work and did as he was instructed, but his quiet demeanor didn't position him as a leader. Being a talented player can be a lonely place.

Especially when you aren't playing up to that talent. And on this Sunday workout, his teammates and coach weren't going to miss an opportunity to let him know about it.

Sunday was going to be a "Run Day." Although it is said working out the day after a game can promote healing, Brian had a little pain in mind for his players. After warmups and some compulsory technical work, Brian was unhappy as usual with the effort of his players. Frustrated and still upset from the loss, Brian told the linebacking crew the last thing they wanted to hear: "Since you guys have been 'half-assers,' I think it's time for some 'half-gassers.'"

The groans from the players let Brian know they knew what was in store for them. A football field is 53 and a 1/3 yards wide. A half-gasser is performed by running down to the sideline and back for 106 and 2/3 total yards. The stopping and re-accelerating can be especially tough on the legs, not to mention your heart feeling like it is going to jump out of your chest.

"Since you all couldn't seem to finish the last 15 minutes of the fourth quarter, we are going to see if you can finish 15 half-gassers in under 18 seconds," yelled Brian with the tone of a dictator. "You will get a generous 45 seconds rest between each rep, so if any one of you doesn't make the time, you'll be sorry."

On Brian's whistle (which he liked to use a lot lately), the athletes took off down and back making the first time. They were still sore from the previous day, but knew they didn't want to suffer more of Brian's wrath if they didn't make it. They didn't call him the "Dark Knight" behind his back for nothing. Brian was, after all, the one who never seemed to run out of punishing exercises to perform.

During the sprints, Brian screamed coaching cues that were far from encouraging:

"Get your asses in gear, ladies! Pick 'em up and put 'em down."

"No wonder we got smoked yesterday by the offense."

"Looks like you are all carrying weights in your pants!"

"Maybe a few less burgers, Johnson! You look like ten pounds of crap in a five-pound bag!"

Even with the negativity, the players kept making the time. But each rep was getting closer to exceeding the dreaded 18-second mark. After each finish, the players would retch as they could barely catch their breath before their 45-second rest was over. Then, everything came to a head with one comment from Brian.

After rep number 14 was completed, a number of the athletes were bent over with their hands on their knees. Marcus was one of those athletes and without thinking, Brian screamed out, "Hey, Chase! Stand up straight before another receiver jumps over you for a game-losing touchdown!"

Even in their fatigued state, the other players let out a chuckle at Marcus's expense. With that, Marcus was beyond angry. When the whistle for the next and final rep blew, unlike the other sprinting athletes, he jogged the final rep. As the whole team watched him after completing the rep well after the allotted time, he stared them down and yelled, "What? I don't hear anyone laughing now!" Then he looked up at Brian and said, "Got any more funny lines … *Coach*?" It was the way he said "coach" that set Brian off. It was as if he was questioning whether he really deserved the title right in front of the team. It stung. And that sting led to rage.

Not one to back down, Brian ran over and got in Marcus's face with a "Now you will run the last rep again alone!"

"No, I won't! I'm DONE!" And with that Marcus turned and walked off the field, to the shock of both the team and Brian. Both Marcus and Brian knew this could signify the end of their careers.

4

Cup of Coffee

After practice, Brian needed somewhere to clear his head before going home. With all the long hours of coaching, there was rarely time to decompress before walking into his own house. As a result, Kelly and the kids would often take the brunt of the emotions that were reflected by the challenges of the day.

To decompress, some of the other coaches would hit the bar. Brian, not being a big drinker, usually chose the Trackside Diner instead. Although Brian wasn't regularly taking in too many calories drinking, the patty melts at Trackside were starting to add up around his waistline.

Brian pulled up, grabbed a seat in a booth and ordered without even looking at the menu. With his head in his hands, he realized aside from his associates at work and family at home, he was alone.

"Is this seat taken?" asked a voice from above Brian.

As he dragged his hands from his eyes and looked up, he saw the same old man from the tunnel standing in front of him.

"Hey, it's you," said Brian, surprised. "I mean, hello and I'm glad I ran into you. Before you say anything, I wanted to apologize for the way I kinda came at you the other night after the game."

"*De nada*, kid," replied the old man. "It was actually my fault. I shouldn't have stirred you up like that. I know how emotional it can be after a loss. I should have known better. I'm just glad you didn't take a swing at me!" the old man said with a laugh.

"Ha!" said Brian. "From the way you responded, I think for some reason you might have been ready for me. But please forgive me for that. And by all means have a seat. God knows I could use a little company right now."

The old man sat down and said, "So tell me what's going on."

This simple question disarmed Brian and he let it all out. The team, Kelly and the kids, the confrontation with Marcus, everything. After patiently listening to Brian's whole story, the old man said, "Thanks for sharing all of that. It took courage to be so honest and open about your challenges. That's the first step toward working on them. Now that we have those out of the way, I think I have a few ideas that could help you if you want."

"Besides the company, I could sure use some help right now, too," replied Brian.

"Great," said the old man. "Then it's time for the first of a number of big questions before I can teach you anything."

"Well, shoot, because I'm ready," said Brian.

"Where is it that you want to go?" said the old man.

"Like to a place on vacation or something?" asked Brian.

"No," said the old man with a smile. "What is your ultimate goal in life? What do you want to achieve? What is it that you really want or want to be known for?"

It had been a long time since Brian had thought about those questions. He had spent so much time working lately, he had forgotten to do any work on himself. Actually, he didn't even know what he wanted anymore. Maybe he never did.

Recognizing he was stumped, the old man said, "Looks like you have a classic problem that affects men … You are afraid to ask for directions! Until you know where you want to go, it's really going to be impossible to help get you there."

"Don't get me wrong," Brian said. "There are things that I want. For instance, I want to make more money and be able to give my family the things they deserve."

"More money?" said the old man.

"Yes," replied Brian.

"Well, how much?" countered the old man and again Brian was stuck with nothing to say. "I think this is a perfect time for an old story I heard that might help you. Would you like to hear it?"

"Do I have a choice?" Brian asked with a smile.

"No, wise guy," said the old man with a wink, and he started in on his story as if he were a narrator of a play. "There was a group of successful alumni from an elite university who got together one day to meet with the professor who had taught them so much many years ago. When they were all assembled, the professor was proud to see many of his most successful students again, but was upset when many of them spent the whole time complaining about the current stress and demands of their high-class lifestyles. That was when the professor realized it was time for another lesson. He asked the students if they would like some of his famous brewed coffee and they all answered, 'yes.' He told them to go into the kitchen and pick one of the coffee cups from his cabinet and get some coffee.

"When the students opened the cabinet they saw a wide range of coffee mugs, from a simple plastic style to regular mugs with cities or quotes on them to vessels that seemed to have great value. Trying to outdo one another, the students started reaching for the best and most expensive mugs, and as they did, some even started arguing over getting a cheaper cup than their colleague. Then, while the smiling professor was watching all of this, he delivered the lesson.

"'My students,' he said, 'what was it that you came in here for again?' Although the students thought it was the cups, one bright student smiled and answered, 'Coffee.' 'Yes,' said the old professor, 'yet it seems you all have forgotten that and are stressing and fighting over the cup instead. Although right now at this stage of your life you may be measuring yourself by having the best things in life, I want you to recognize that this material desire is also creating your stress and unhappiness. The important things you really want from life are like coffee. The cup you select doesn't add to or subtract from the quality of the coffee. In fact, it only covers it up, just like the houses and cars and careers you try to surround yourself with. So, I'm not telling you not to chase the finer things in life. I'm just reminding you not to lose sight of enjoying the aspects of your life that you consider the coffee.'"

"That's a powerful story there," said Brian.

"Ha, don't get me started," said the old man. "I have a lot of those. Telling stories is a great way to get your point across. Speaking of points, you see," said the old man, "you don't have direction. You are just like most people out there. They all have the same wishes and dreams for things that end up causing them stress while they miss out on the important things in life. News flash, kid. Everyone wants more money and to take care of their family. They all want a nice house and to travel and maybe to have some fame, too. In order for any of that to happen, you have to be crystal clear on the thing that is going to get you fired up to make it happen."

"Well, how do I do that?" asked Brian.

"With what I call a little enthusiasm adjustment, slick," said the old man. "Success, as I have learned, is all about enthusiasm. You have to rediscover your passion; meaning what it is you are enthusiastic about."

"Sounds easy enough," said Brian.

"If it was easy," the old man said, "the world would be filled with a lot more upbeat and satisfied people, son."

"Well, what do I have to do?" asked Brian as he made his way through his patty melt. "At this point I'm open to ideas, and if you haven't noticed, I sure could benefit from a little more enthusiasm right now."

"That's for sure," said the old man.

"Really?" said Brian.

"Just calling it like I see it, kid," said the old man. "It just so happens you are in luck. I think I have the information you need to turn yourself around. But I am going to be honest. Working with me will involve some hard work."

"I've never been afraid of putting in some extra time," said Brian.

"Good," said the old man. "Then before I let you get back to your family, here is your first assignment," as he pulled a folded-up paper from his pocket and stared right into Brian's eyes. "On this paper is the most important thing that will direct your life. Actually, it contains all the direction and motivation you will ever need."

Eagerly, Brian took the paper from his hand, unfolded it and opened it to the blank side. Quickly flipping it over, he noticed the other side was blank, too, except for one word in the top corner: enthusIASM. With a confused expression, he looked from the paper to the old man.

"Oh, tonight your job is to write down that most important thing. I can't tell you what it is. I'm not a magician, you know," said the old man with a laugh. "But that one word on the paper is your reminder what to do. Enthusiasm is a Greek word. The first part of the word, *enthus*, means to be filled with spirit. So that is what you are on fire about. The IASM is an acronym I use to stand for I AM SOLD MYSELF. Those letters represent what you really believe in. And when you really believe in something, that energy is apparent to everyone else around you, too. When you really believe in something heart and soul, other people have no choice but to start to believe it, too. Tonight I want you to really soul search about what it is you love to do and why you love to do it. Once you figure out that intersection of your passion and your purpose, I think I will be able to help you."

The old man stood up to leave and Brian said, "Thanks so much for listening tonight. Sorry to weigh you down with my problems. I just realized I never got to ask you anything. I guess that was pretty selfish of me."

"No worries, Brian," said the old man. "I wasn't here tonight to talk about me. That's a lesson I have a feeling I will teach you another time. Speaking of other times, let me know when you are open to go over your answers."

Worried he might not see the old man again, Brian said, "I'm usually booked during the season, but how does lunch tomorrow at 1 p.m. sound? The cafeteria isn't much, but it will be my treat."

"Sounds good, and I'll see you then. Don't forget the paper," said the old man.

"Sure thing," said Brian.

"And before I go, here's assignment #2. That kid you upset today could be feeling as bad as you are right now.

Before he goes and does something drastic that you will both regret, I think you should write him and apologize."

"Apologize?" said Brian incredulously.

"Yes," said the old man. "And make sure he shows up for practice after our lunch tomorrow. Trust me on this one."

"Okay. I'll text him now. Thanks again for your time. Come to think of it, I didn't even catch your name," said Brian as the old man started to walk away with a slight limp.

"You can just call me coach," the old man answered. And with that, he walked out to the ringing of the bell on the diner door.

5

Enthusiasm

That evening, Brian pulled into his driveway feeling less stressed than usual. Inspired from his meeting at the diner, he felt compelled to take action on the homework the old man had given him. After texting Marcus a serious apology and request to be at practice tomorrow, Brian turned off his phone and made a commitment to stay a little more present with his daughters and Kelly. When he walked in, he was greeted by his girls. He had forgotten how good it felt to see them come running and yell, "Daddy's home!" when he walked in the door. They had a nice dinner and conversation, and even Kelly seemed a little more at ease than usual. In a weird way, Brian already felt a little more in control because of the old coach he had met. And when he thought about it, the old coach hadn't done more than listen and give him an assignment.

"So, what's gotten into you?" Kelly asked.

"What do you mean?" Brian answered.

"After that loss yesterday, you would usually be hitting game film and stressing over next week's game. You seem a little … different. Is everything okay?" Kelly inquired.

"Sure, babe," Brian assured her. "I just met an unusual coach today and he gave me an interesting assignment. I guess it already has me thinking, and that thinking has slightly changed my attitude, too."

"What was the assignment?" asked his oldest daughter Jenny. "Is it like he gave you some homework?"

"That's exactly what he did," Brian answered. "And just like you, tonight I am going to make sure I get it all done."

"So he's your teacher?" asked his youngest daughter Jaime.

"Ha! Well, I guess he is," said Brian realizing his kids were always listening. "And I have a strange feeling he has a lot to teach me. At least I hope he does."

"I thought you knew everything already, Daddy," said Jaime.

"No, Jaime," said Brian. "Every Daddy always has more to learn."

That night, Brian kept his commitment and was more present. It felt good to focus on the girls; they were growing up right before his eyes. And after teeth were brushed, a story was read, and they were tucked in, Brian let Kelly know about the assignment and asked her what she thought his answers might be. Kelly always seemed to know him even better than he knew himself. Her answers revolved more around service and helping others than football. She reminded him of his previous volunteer work and other coaching jobs before he got so "serious." This was the inspiration Brian needed before he started to jot down his own ideas.

After Kelly went to bed (she had to get up early to get the girls off to school and then to work) Brian pulled out the paper and concentrated on the word *enthusIASM*. As he thought about what he really loved to do, he remembered a conversation with one of his former athletes who signed a huge contract in the NFL. Even though the player had more money than he would ever need, he was unhappy. Years later when he and Brian were talking at a team reunion, he remembered the player remarking, "24 hours is a long time to have nothing to do. You can only spend so much time on a beach or playing golf."

That comment always stuck with Brian. So, he decided that money was not what was firing him up. After all, if it was, he would be involved in another profession. There had to be something deeper that would get him up early and keep him up late. Brian thought the easy answer would be football, and although it was still one of his greatest passions, he could see that he was not sold on football being his purpose. As he remembered, the instructions were to find the intersection of his passion and his purpose. Perhaps when he did this, the money might appear, too.

At the kitchen table, Brian kept digging deeper into what really drove him. Inspired by some of Kelly's answers, he reflected on his past and the people who had inspired him the most in his life. He realized immediately that his father had not lived his passion and purpose. His dad worked hard for 40 years and made decent money, but obviously did it solely to provide for him and his family, not because he loved it.

The person who seemed to have found the inter-section was actually his high school track coach. Coach Scarola was always on fire and never seemed to have a bad day. Although he surely didn't make the big dollars, he never seemed to be without, and Brian realized he always wanted to be as well liked as that coach. In fact, it was Coach Scarola who inspired Brian to be a coach in the first place. That was when inspiration struck. Brian realized his own passion didn't come from making money or football, it came from helping people. And how was he best able to help people? Through coaching! Coaching also passed the IASM test—I AM SOLD MYSELF—for Brian. He believed that coaching was important and knew his own life would be radically different if he hadn't been blessed with some of the coaches he'd had. Satisfied with his answer, he wrote *Helping others through coaching* on his sheet under the word *enthusIASM*. And then he wrote a note to himself as his goal: *I want to be a better coach*. Somehow his mind felt clearer and like a weight had been lifted as he went to bed.

Brian felt like he had taken a few steps forward. Little did he know he was going to be knocked back a few more the next day.

6

Ultimatum

The next morning, when Brian turned on his phone, there were two texts that concerned him. One he received and one he didn't. The first was from the head coach of the team requesting they have a quick meeting at 6 a.m. The second was that Brian could tell Marcus had read his text, but did not respond. Brian wasn't sure which one worried him the most, but he knew neither was good news. No matter what, he was looking forward to lunch with the old coach and hoped he still had a pass to the cafeteria by the time lunch rolled around.

The head coach, Rick Olsen, was a hard-working coach with a long history of successful programs at four different universities. Now feeling the pressure from the school administrators for some victories, he too was pressing his staff to get the most out of what they had.

Coach Olsen had brought with him a number of his former assistant coaches and instituted the core values and culture that he had successfully used at the previous schools. Brian knew it would take a few more seasons to get complete buy-in from the players and worried they could all be gone before that happened. He was sure Coach Olsen knew it, too.

Coach Olsen and Brian had a good relationship, but with all the demands of the game at this level, there wasn't much time to be mentored with personal time or grow as a football coach. The goal was to win games, recruit better players, and keep repeating that cycle in hopes to improve to a Top 25 or Top 10 ranking. The way things were looking this season, both of those were long shots at best.

Brian made his way to Coach Olsen's office, passed his secretary and knocked on the door.

"Come on in and sit down," Coach Olsen said.

Brian sat on the plush leather chair where many an athlete and coach before him had either been criticized or praised. The room was filled with memorabilia of past football victories. Having had a number of these meetings, Brian knew it was best to sit back and listen.

"Glad you're here, Brian," said Coach Olsen. "With the season upon us and a loss behind us, I'm not going to sugarcoat anything. You know I like you and you also know I'm a straight shooter. I consider you a valuable part of this staff and brought you in here to do a job. Quite frankly, you and your athletes are not performing at the level I had hoped, and I want to help. You aren't spending time around any of the other coaches, either. I get the feeling you aren't completely on board with the team. I feel this way because lately you seem a little distracted and, to be honest, downright ornery. I know the pressures of this position and having a young family are tough. But hey, I didn't bring you in here to yell at you, but to see if everything is okay. So, is everything okay?"

Brian shrugged and thought about his answer. After the initial angst that his demeanor was starting to be apparent to everyone, he decided to open up. He told the coach that his marriage was strained and he thought both work and home life were affecting each other. Coach Olsen did listen, and, having worked his way up the same ranks, was sympathetic to the young coach. He gave him a few pieces of advice, but the main idea revolved around this business "being tough to have a family." Brian was at least thankful the coach was trying to understand, but the end of the conversation still worried him.

"Thanks for being up front and showing a little vulnerability, Brian," said Coach Olsen.

"Thank you for understanding, Coach," replied Brian.

"Well, don't forget," said Coach Olsen. "Understanding is not the same as excusing. You still have a job to do and that involves fixing what is going on with both of your teams … this one and your family. You need to figure out how to improve in both of those areas. You know that football jobs will come and go, but your family only happens once. Now that I know the deal, I'm going to check in and hold you more accountable."

"Understood, and thanks again, Coach," said Brian with his eyes down and focused on the big desk in front of him.

As Brian was leaving the meeting, he knew he had been put on notice. Coach Olsen's final request, however, let him know that more than just Brian's temper was out in the open.

"And I didn't think it was the time to cover it now, Brian," said Coach Olsen, "but I heard about the issue with Marcus at the end of practice yesterday. The kid could really use your help, not your anger. I believe he's as good a person as he is a player. I'm hoping you're going to help pull both of those out of him. That is, after all, your job."

"Roger that, Coach," said Brian. And as he tapped the piece of folded paper in his pocket, he cracked a small smile and said, "I am already on it."

7

The Right Target

Following his meeting with Coach Olsen, Brian carried out his regular duties until lunch. The folded paper in his pocket was his reminder about his lunch date and a reminder that he really did want to be a better coach in order to help people.

Brian had to hustle across campus to the cafeteria, and when he got there a couple minutes late, the old coach was already at the door waiting for him. They shook hands (the old coach had an impressive grip Brian noticed didn't release until Brian did first), grabbed some food, and had a seat at a table for two looking out on the hustle of campus life.

"Let me guess," said the old coach. "The X's and O's were holding you up?"

"You got it, Coach," Brian said with a smile. "Sounds like you know a thing or two about football. Got any secret defenses to share?"

"Nah," laughed the old coach. "You aren't missing that stuff. And you have probably forgotten more than I know there. I'm here to teach you about the secrets you don't know. And hopefully that coaching is a lot more than the X's and O's. My secrets are actually about who those X's and O's are and how to get the most out of them."

"That makes sense," said Brian. "I've spent so many years focused on the nuances of the game thinking that was the secret to being more valuable in my industry. I guess I'm starting to realize there is more to coaching than coverages and schemes."

"Good thought there, kid," said the old coach. "Sounds like in addition to the challenges you have with direction, you have what I call a little 'targeting' problem. Want to hear another interesting story?"

"Sure," said Brian, who, like everyone, loved a good story, especially the way the old coach told them.

"This one starts in the state of New Jersey with an Olympic athlete," the old coach began. "And no, I am not talking about Carl Lewis or a famous Olympic sport like track and field, gymnastics, or swimming. This athlete's name was Matt Emmons, and he was in the lesser-known Olympic sport of rifle shooting. Matt had been one of the best in the world for years leading up to the 2004 Olympics in Athens. He was shooting in the three-position event in which he would fire from his stomach, knees, and standing at the target, which was positioned 50 meters away. With only one shot to go and so far out in gold medal position, all Matt had to do was hit the target to secure the gold. As many riflemen do, Matt slowed his breathing to make the final shot in order to precisely squeeze the trigger in between his heartbeats so as not to make a mistake. Then he squeezed the trigger and BANG!" the old coach said and slapped his thigh for emphasis. "He didn't just hit the target with a mediocre shot. He hit it dead solid perfect."

Then the old coach paused and said, "And with that perfect shot, he moved from first place into eighth place and out of the medals."

With that statement, Brian, who had been listening intently, furrowed his brow in confusion and tilted his head to the right. Then the old coach delivered the lesson.

"Do you know what happened? Do you know what Matt Emmons did? He shot the *wrong target*!" the old man exclaimed.

"What? No way!" replied Brian, shocked.

"Yes, way," countered the old coach. "He took perfect aim. It was just on the target that was one lane over."

"Oh, man!" said Brian. "That had to be tough to recover from."

"Well, not any tougher than recovering from all the wrong targets you're aiming at right now, kid," responded the old coach.

"What do you mean?"

"Well," answered the old coach, "You just said you're putting in a ton of time on X's and O's, yet you are having less success on the field. You also complained about gaining some weight, yet you are sitting here eating something that probably isn't going to help." (Brian was eating a double cheeseburger and fries compared to the grilled chicken salad and broccoli of the coach.) "And you have told me you feel your marriage is in some jeopardy, yet it sounds like you are spending less time home than ever."

"I didn't think of it like that," said Brian. "Well, that story has me thinking and I have to tell you, I had a meeting with Coach Olsen today and if I don't start turning things around with the team, I may be having to target myself for another job."

"Don't worry about that just yet, kid," said the old man. "I think I can help you. And getting you clear on your targeting is first making sure you are clear on exactly what that target is. You see, most people, just like Matt, aren't clear on the right target. And without that clarity, they end up spending their lives unsuccessful, unsatisfied, or both. Clarity, above all, is true power."

"So, how do I get more clarity?" asked Brian.

"Well," said the old coach, "Hopefully you completed your homework assignment from last night?"

Proud of the fact he had done the work and satisfied with his discovery, Brian pulled out the folded paper from his pocket and before he could even show the old coach what he had written, he felt compelled to start explaining.

"You see, Coach," Brian began, "I thought about what really fired me up and I realized that it wasn't just football or a house or a new car. I guess I really got clear on the fact that I get a rush when I've helped someone. And then I saw the way I do that best is by coaching someone. So that's why I wrote my intersection is *Helping others through coaching*, and I think my goal is to become a better coach."

"I'm proud of you," said the old coach as he smiled at Brian, letting him take the statement in before giving him a fist bump. Brian smiled back and realized it had been a long time since someone had said those words to him. He actually felt a boost in energy until the old coach said, "But, as your coach, I think you can make your target a little more clear here. 'Better' is such a nebulous term. It's kind of like 'more' or 'nicer.' I want more money or a nicer life are not clear targets. And when you are unclear, you lack the power and drive to achieve them. I suggest you go for something bigger than better. Do you have any idea what is bigger than better?"

"Best?" answered Brian.

"Yes!" exclaimed the old coach, who seemed to have a harder time than Brian covering up his enthusiasm. "And my challenge to you isn't to be the best coach on this staff or even the best in college football. I think you need to shoot for bigger. How about for being the best coach in the world!"

"The best in the world?" questioned Brian. "Isn't that a little hard to measure, too?"

"Sure," said the old coach. "I agree it's probably impossible for the world to elect the best coach, but in trying to always become the best, you will ceaselessly learn and train to improve your skills. You will never become complacent or think you've made it. Many people do this and the minute they reach a small goal like getting better, they stop growing. And that is actually when they start going backward. I believe the pursuit of your best never lets you rest."

"Ha," laughed Brian. "I guess you're right."

"Don't guess, son," said the old coach. "Be sure about it. That's what clarity is all about. So, cross out that old goal on your paper and add the new one, if you don't mind. As I learned long ago, it's better to 'ink' it than 'think' it."

Brian liked how the old coach was like a fortune cookie always ready with a line or idea that he needed to hear. And Brian did as the old coach requested. He crossed out *I want to be a better coach* and replaced it with *I want to be the best coach in the world.*

With lunch finished and Brian having to get to practice, he knew he was pressed for time, but he had really enjoyed spending time with the old coach. There was something familiar about him that not only made Brian feel better, but also made him feel like he could and would become more. The old coach was really opening his mind and guiding him to imagine more possibilities. Maybe that was also a part of what coaching was all about.

As they exchanged goodbyes, Brian asked, "Coach, do you have any advice for how to handle things with Marcus Chase? He didn't respond when I texted him to apologize, and if he hopefully comes to practice today, I want to start patching things up."

"He'll be there today," said the old coach. "I've watched the kid practice and play. He just needs some people on his side … just like you do. My advice is to copy everything I've been doing with you over the last couple of days."

"So should I ask him to lunch at the cafeteria tomorrow?" asked Brian.

"No, silly," laughed the old coach. "Follow everything we have done since our first confrontation. You should seek him out and apologize and show him you want to help. Then you should give him a blank piece of paper for him to write down what excites him and his big goal. *Then* you ask him to lunch to discuss it."

"Got it, Coach. And thanks again," said Brian.

"My pleasure," replied the old coach. "Will you have time to stop by Trackside again tonight? I know it cuts into your time at home, but I think you're going to need to understand another concept about DIRECTION now that you have your targeting on point."

"I can swing by for sure," said Brian. "And I might even order something a little healthier tonight, too."

"Good idea, kid," said the old coach with a smile. "Looks like an old dog can learn new tricks after all."

8

Eating Crow

Brian had some coaches' meetings and film work to get done before practice. Although many of the coaches often worked together, lately he had been working solo. He was getting his job done, but he knew he was going to have to be a better contributor to the staff and team.

He also knew he wanted to talk to Marcus before the players all got out on the practice field. If there was one thing he had learned, it was the importance of praising in public and criticizing in private. Since he wasn't sure if Marcus was going to be aggressive again or not, he wanted to make sure he kept this meeting between just the two of them.

Brian made his way into the locker room and was relieved to see that like the old coach predicted, Marcus was in fact at his locker and dressing for practice. When Marcus looked up and saw him, Brian could tell by his reaction that he was as nervous to talk to his coach as Brian was to talk to his player. Marcus put his head down and pretended to focus on tying his shoes.

"Hey, Marcus," said Brian. "I hope you saw my text. I wanted to let you know I'm sorry for what I said yesterday. Can we talk in private for a minute?"

"Am I in trouble?" asked Marcus.

"No," answered Brian. "I just wanted to explain my actions yesterday and hopefully give you an idea how to get you playing at your best."

"So are you saying I'm not playing well?" asked Marcus, crossing his arms defensively.

"That's not what I am saying, Marcus," said Brian, standing in an open posture like the old coach did, with his hands at his sides and his palms open. "I just want us to get on the same page so I can do my best to help you.

I actually think the trouble is with me and I have been letting you down."

With that response, Marcus uncrossed his arms, and he and Brian walked over to a film room and sat down. Brian again apologized for his comment and stated that it wasn't something a good coach would do. He also promised that it wouldn't happen again and that he would like to do more to help Marcus play at his best.

Because Marcus and Brian didn't have much of a relationship beyond coach and player, Marcus didn't have any reason not to trust Brian, but he was still skeptical. But he knew that the way he had been playing the last few years, anything that could make him better would be worth a shot.

"Before I show you any linebacker techniques or talk any more defense with you, Marcus, I want to start with something different," said Brian as he pulled out a blank piece of paper. "This is an exercise that can help you get better, and I know it can help because it really helped me."

"What's the exercise?" asked Marcus.

"Well, I want to know a little bit more about what you want from football and why," said Brian. "If I could get you to help me understand your goals, maybe I can better help you to achieve them."

"So what do I have to do?" asked Marcus.

"Tonight I want you to imagine this paper is the most important piece of paper in the world," said Brian. "I want you to think about and write down what it is you are most passionate about and I want you to spend time thinking what is really driving you to be your best. Then we can talk about your answers tomorrow and together come up with a plan on how to do it."

Although this seemed a little "touchy-feely" to Marcus (and he had heard stuff like this from the number of coaches he had before) there was something about the way Brian authentically sounded like he wanted to help. With nothing to lose, Marcus accepted the assignment and agreed he would do his best.

"Now remember," Brian said, "This isn't something to take lightly. I want you to really spend time jotting down ideas until you come up with what you think is the big answer. Just like for me, this could take you some time and a number of revisions. But I promise the work will be worth it. And that answer you discover might just surprise you.

"Okay," said Marcus. "I'll do it … and one more thing," he continued, with the first smile Brian had seen in some time. "Maybe you'll eventually show me how to stop a guy trying to jump over me?"

"Ha," said Brian. "You got it."

9

The Real Definition

After their conversation, Brian and Marcus made their way out to the practice field together. Even though the other players were shocked to see them getting along, the grueling physical and mental demands of practice had them quickly forgetting the confrontation that happened the day before. The next few hours were filled with the alternation of drills, whistles, and bodies moving in the formations that would be expected for the big game on the upcoming Saturday. Even with the long practice and fall heat still lingering, Brian felt invigorated, and his players seemed to feed off his newfound energy, too. Brian knew there were some lessons in all of this and he couldn't wait to get over to the Trackside Diner after practice.

The old coach was sitting in the same booth from the evening before as Brian entered and walked over.

"Looks like this could be our usual spot, huh, coach?" said Brian.

"Ha, yes. Good to see you, Brian," said the old coach. "How did everything go today?"

Brian updated the coach on the meeting with Marcus and how well practice seemed to go. The coach was not surprised.

"Well, kid," the old coach said, "sounds like you got a little lesson on how a coach spells the word *CARE*."

"What do you mean, Coach?"

"Simple," said the old coach. "Any coach worth his or her salt knows the way to spell care is T-I-M-E. You spent a little time on Marcus, gave him a little extra attention, and look at the result!"

"I like that one, Coach," said Brian. "I guess I could probably spell that one out a little better at home, too."

"For sure, kid. Coaching and parenting and being a boss or a friend are all the same thing. And anyway, it isn't your fault if you aren't getting it all done correctly right now."

"What do you mean?" asked Brian.

"I mean how many classes did you ever have on being the best coach in the world? Or how many books have you read on the subject?" asked the old coach.

"Well, none, come to think of it."

"Exactly," said the old coach. "So nothing up to this point is your fault. You've just been trying to find your way and probably just emulating other coaches you've had in the past. Well, I have some good and bad news for you."

"What's the good news?"

"The good news is that after today's lesson, you are going to be as crystal clear on what it means to be a coach as you now are about your passion and purpose," said the old coach.

"Well then, what's the bad news?"

"The bad news is that after today, if you mess it up, it is your fault," the old coach said with a smile.

The two ordered their food and the old coach seemed happy Brian had chosen to go with a healthier salad and water. While they waited for the food to arrive, the old coach started his next master class on coaching.

"If you're going to be the best coach in the world," the old coach began, "you first have to understand what the word *coach* really means. So before I tell you what I believe, I want to know what you think. Brian, what do you think it means to be a coach?"

Brian was surprised to realize that he had never really thought about this before. Although he was called a coach and wore the name on the back of many of his shirts over the years, aside from a position of authority or using a whistle and title to get people to do what he wanted them to do, he really wasn't sure of his exact job description. He knew he was currently measured in wins and losses, but he thought being a coach had to be more than that. Instead of answering right away, he sat thinking, hoping the old coach would continue with the lesson before he answered with something that made him either look or feel stupid.

"Cat got your tongue?" asked the old coach after a few moments.

"Well, you kind of have me stumped," Brian admitted. "I know there are a lot of facets to coaching, like teaching and motivation, but I'm having a hard time condensing my ideas down into something that works. Coaching is, after all, pretty complex, isn't it?"

"Ha. That's the trouble with people these days," the old coach said. "They take a simple idea and try to make it too complex. Then they do nothing. Take nutrition, for instance. People can talk about a hundred different diets or exotic foods, but it really comes down to controlling calories and putting the right foods in your mouth. Anyone telling you different is trying to confuse you or sell you something. There ain't no label on an apple, right?"

"I can agree with that. I had a coach once who told me mastery isn't making the simple things complex; it is making the complex things simple," said Brian.

"Sounds like a smart guy."

"Yeah, he was, come to think of it," said Brian. "Now if you can make eating right so easy, what do you have on coaching?"

"Like I said," said the old coach, "the first step is having a working definition of what the word *coach* means. Then once you are clear on the word, you can make sure you are clear about carrying out your job. Anything else is guessing. Now to begin, have you ever flown in the back of a plane?"

"Sure," answered Brian. "We have to fly for games all the time."

"And when you sit in the back of the plane," queried the old coach, "what do they call it?"

"They say you ride in coach." said Brian.

"Correct," said the old coach. "And if you sit in the back of a train, what do they call it?"

"They call that riding in coach, too," answered Brian.

"Right again!" said the old coach. "And do you have any idea what they call buses in England?"

"Let me guess … coaches?" said Brian with a smile.

"You are really on fire tonight," said the old coach. "But now here is the tougher question: Do you know why all those things are called a coach?"

"Now you've got me," answered Brian.

"This is where it gets cool," said the old coach. "Would you believe the word actually originated from a village in Hungary?"

"That's not the answer I was expecting," said Brian.

"Well it's true. And here's why. In the fifteenth century, skilled artisans in the village of Kocs started producing the best horse-drawn carriages. Word spread of their advanced design all over Europe, and the word *coach* started to be used for this mode of transportation. After other methods of transportation appeared, they kept the name 'coach' going. That's why you've heard of a stagecoach and mentioned you've ridden in coach. Pretty cool, huh?"

"Sounds great and all, but what does a stagecoach have to do with me becoming the best coach in the world?" asked Brian.

"That brings me to the definition I want you to understand for the word *coach*. Once you understand it completely, you will have everything you need to make sure you're on the right path. I can promise that once I understood the word, this definition never let me down."

"Then please end the suspense!" smiled Brian, who was really interested in hearing what the old coach had to say. The old coach had a way about him of keeping a person's interest.

"Well," said the old coach, "It took me a long time to learn this definition. In fact, I learned over about 15 years that there are three separate pieces in the description for the word *coach*. And only once you understand and use all three together, will you have a shot at being the best coach in the world."

"Now that you understand the origin of the word *coach*," he continued, "the first part is the easiest and yet most profound. Since the word *coach* was meant to signify transportation, I made my own interpretation for coaching that has never failed me. It is so important, I want you to write it down on something valuable."

With that, the old coach pulled out a small book from under the table. Brian could see the 5-by-3-inch leather cover and inch-thick of paper was held closed by a black band. What drew Brian's attention wasn't the size of the book, but the shiny gold color of the durable cover. It glistened like some of the helmets he had seen over the years.

"This is for me?" asked Brian.

"Yes," replied the old coach. "This could be the most valuable coaching book you ever own."

Brian eagerly pulled the black band over the top of the pages and was surprised to see all the pages were blank.

"I thought you said this was a valuable coaching book," said Brian, slightly confused.

"Yes," replied the old coach with a smile. "After you fill it with all the things you need to be the best coach in the world, that is. Think of it more like a notebook. So, first, at the top of the first page, write the word *coach*."

Brian looked a little skeptical. "Why do I have to write it down?" he asked.

"As I learned," said the old coach with another signature wink, "your mind may forget, but the paper will always remember. Use that notebook to write down any good coaching ideas you get from time to time. You will see it will become the most important book you own someday."

"Now," instructed the old coach, "for the first line under the word *coach*, I want you to write the words, *to take you somewhere*."

Brian wrote those with a smile. "I like that," he said. "That really is the simple job description of a great coach, isn't it?"

"Well, kid," the old coach replied, "if you only knew that part, you could still be lousy and call yourself a coach. As I learned the hard way, that first part of the definition of a coach is not enough to be the best. Let me ask you about some of the coaches from your past. Did you ever have a good coach?"

"Well, sure," answered Brian. "I had a lot of good coaches."

"Then tell me about the best one you ever had."

"That's easy," replied Brian. "I had a track coach in seventh grade who really changed my life."

"Now we're talking," said the old coach. "So tell me a little about that."

"Well," said Brian with a smile, "I wasn't always the strapping athlete you see before you right now, Coach."

"Ha," said the old coach. "Let's stick with the salads and broccoli a little longer before you go there, son. Now get back to your story."

"When I was in seventh grade," Brian began, "I wasn't very good in school. In fact, I was doing poorly. Being young for my grade, I was behind in school and really not feeling good about myself. I was a latchkey kid, meaning I was alone a lot because both of my parents worked to support our family. Not that they didn't support me in things, but I have to admit I often felt on my own. My only outlet was sports. At that time my favorite sport was baseball. But when I went for the seventh grade tryouts at school, the coach told us at the meeting that no seventh-graders would get to try out since they already had enough eighth- and ninth-graders trying out for the team. I was devastated at the thought of no sports for the spring. On my way out of the meeting, though, there was this coach standing outside the doorway. And he told every kid walking out the same thing:

"'Hey, kid, I heard there's no baseball, but you look *perfect* for track!'

"Although most kids kept walking, when he told me I looked perfect for track, that got my attention. At the time I didn't think I was perfect at anything. And I asked the only thing a 12-year-old could think of: 'Track?' I said. And he said 'Yeah!' So I said, 'What's that?'"

"Ha, ha," laughed the old coach. "Sounds like that guy was pretty passionate about track and field. So what happened after that?"

"He was passionate, for sure," said Brian. "And that passion got me to go out for track the next day. Not only was I on the team for the next six years, but he developed me both physically and mentally. He taught me a lot about training and made sure I got my grades up. He was also the one who believed I could play football at a higher level. And being an assistant football coach, he was a big reason I played at the next level."

"Wow, sounds like this coach really took you somewhere," said the old coach.

"He sure did," said Brian. "And we're still in touch today on social media after all these years. I think I have a better appreciation for that first part of the definition of 'coach' now. What's the second part?"

"Well, teaching the second part always involves a little less enjoyable walk down memory lane," said the old coach, pausing to make sure the point sank in. "Now I want you to tell me about one of the worst coaches you had."

At this moment, Brian realized he had forgotten he'd had a number of bad coaches in his life, too. Whether it was not putting in the effort, not looking at the potential he had, or just more interested in collecting a paycheck, Brian realized he may have had more bad coaches than good ones. Even with this new understanding, there was one bad coaching experience that stood out. And not until that moment did Brian realize that it also happened in seventh grade.

"This is interesting, Coach," said Brian. "Only a few months before I met my coach after the baseball tryouts,

I had a really bad experience at my seventh-grade soccer tryouts."

"Really?" asked the old coach. "Please tell me more about it."

"When I was growing up," Brian said, "I was always a fast kid, even though I had a stocky build. Whether it was backyard races or playing on the sports field, my speed always gave me opportunities for success. I started soccer when I was six years old and that speed always led to me scoring goals. As a result, I played the front line and enjoyed the offensive side of the game. When I got to seventh grade, though, there was a new coach in charge of the team and I was a new athlete at the school. Tryouts for seventh grade weren't what you might think. There were no running or technical evaluations. Instead, this new coach had an evaluation method all his own. What he did was line up all the new kids and ask them to state their name and the position they played. He would listen to the name and position and then send them in the direction of that position. But for me, he did something different. When I said, 'My name is Brian Knight, and I play center; I like to score goals,' he kind of just looked at me and laughed. Then he patted me on the belly and said, 'Go over there. You play defense now, Chubby.'"

"Ugh. I bet that was a real hit with the team," said the old coach.

"You said it," Brian said. "Not only was I humiliated by the coach, but it also got worse because things weren't as PC back then. Kids were laughing and you can only imagine what my new nickname was."

"Lemme guess," said the old coach. "Chubby?"

"Hey, come on, Coach," Brian grinned. "I'm still a little sensitive about that. But yeah, that was my new nickname, and as a 12-year-old, I wasn't going to put up with it. So, unfortunately, because of one mean comment at the expense of a little kid, I quit the sport of soccer forever."

"I'm sorry to hear that. But I'm glad to hear that you not only understand the power a coach has on the life of someone else, but also that you should completely understand the next part of the definition I want you to write down. But before you write it, let me ask you: Did that soccer coach take you somewhere?"

"Not at all," said Brian immediately.

"Don't answer too fast there, Brian. He most certainly did! You mentioned he led you to quit the sport and probably to a place where you felt less of yourself."

"Yeah, I guess you're right," answered Brian.

"Again, there's no guessing here when we are searching for clarity," reminded the old coach. "Both your track coach and soccer coach took you somewhere. Any good or bad coach can do that. But the next thing you'll add to our definition of a coach makes all the difference. So, after the first four words *to take you somewhere*, I want you to write the next four words, *you want to go*."

In that moment, the lightbulb went on for Brian. He started to see clearly that a coach's job is to help someone get where they want to go, not to do anything or put up any roadblocks or resistance to stop them from the destination. He also quickly realized he had not always been heeding this job description and was a little saddened by the thought of his own coaching lately.

"Don't worry," said the old coach, reading Brian's body language. "Like I said, nothing up to this point has been your fault, since you were never clear on the job description of a coach."

Brian nodded, but there were faces of past athletes appearing in his mind who he realized he could have helped more and some that he was the reason why they didn't reach their goals.

"Man," said Brian. "This has really shown me that most people get a lot of good and bad coaches in their life. And I see now I've *been* both of them, too."

"That's why we're going over this," said the old coach. "From now on you get a choice of which kind of coach you want to be."

"I know that answer, Coach," said Brian. "I want to be a good one."

To that, the coach just sat quietly and raised an eyebrow in question until Brian got the point.

"I mean I want to be the best one!" said Brian with a smile. That answer made the old coach smile, too.

"Well," said the old coach, "in order to be the best, you still need the last part of your job description. Although 'To take someone where they want to go' works fine, I found over many years there's one last piece that makes the real difference. Let me ask you about this kid Marcus again. Didn't you say he was a top recruit out of high school?"

"Yes," answered Brian. "He was one of the top high school players in the country. I, like a lot of people, have been pretty disappointed he hasn't played up to the potential we saw back then."

"What kind of potential are we talking about?"

"When we recruited him," said Brian, "He was so big and strong, it was like he was in on every tackle on every play."

"So he was a bit like a man amongst boys out there?" asked the old coach.

"That was exactly it," said Brian. "But since he's been here, he's done enough to start, but he hasn't shown the same level of dominance that he did."

"Did you ever think that just being big and strong isn't enough to dominate at this level?" asked the old coach.

"What do you mean?" asked Brian.

"Well, he isn't playing against boys anymore," replied the old coach. "At the college level, everyone has size and strength. This is when technical knowledge and skill can also be a separator. In high school you can get away with pure athleticism or hitting puberty earlier. But here, you have to constantly be developing your skills to separate yourself. Have you been working on those skills with Marcus? Is he a much different player since high school?"

"To be honest," said Brian thoughtfully, "I guess he isn't. We've been relying on that athleticism and although he has hit the weight room hard, I haven't given him all I can to make him the best player he could be. In fact, since I wasn't the fastest or the strongest when I played, I actually had to learn those skills you're talking about."

"And did you learn them on your own?" asked the old coach.

"No," said Brian. "It was my college coach who really spent the time with me to show me what he knew."

"Now you understand the third piece of the definition of the word *coach*," said the old coach with a grin. "Few people can reach their dreams alone. We all need help, and that's what coaching is all about. So, for the final six words of the definition, I want you to write *when you can't get there yourself* on the paper."

At that moment, Brian wrote down the final words in his notebook to make the definition complete:

coach
to take you somewhere
you want to go
when you can't get there yourself

Brian read and re-read the words and thought about them as he finished his salad in silence. He really liked what he saw in the little golden notebook. He realized that if every interaction he had with someone he coached always got them a little closer to where they wanted to go that they couldn't get to themselves, his life would be a lot more positive. And that wasn't just on the sports field. This definition was a great rule for life. He immediately understood that he hadn't been living this job description either on the field or at home. In many ways he was doing the opposite with Kelly and the kids. This epiphany was a breakthrough moment.

"I think this is really going to help me, Coach," said Brian.

"I *know* it is. And it's going to help you help a lot more people, too. Now it's time for you to get outta here and put the job description to work at home," answered the old coach, seeming to read his mind.

"Thanks so much for this notebook and ... for everything," said Brian.

"Thank me by putting the ideas I'm giving you into practice," said the old coach. "Knowledge really doesn't mean squat. Success in life is all about taking some action. Speaking of action, now that you are eating a little better, I'm hoping you can join me for a little workout tomorrow morning? It won't take long, but now that you're a little clearer about your job, I have your next lesson in mind on how to be the best. What do you say about 4:30 a.m. at the practice field?"

Already feeling a little better from having a healthy meal, Brian couldn't argue that he really hadn't been paying attention to his health lately. "I think that's another target I need to better aim at, Coach. I'll be there," said Brian.

"Good. Bring your sneakers and some water," said the old coach.

"Anything else?" asked Brian.

"Yeah," said the old coach with a sinister smile. "Bring a lunch pail, because you are going to work!"

At the same time Brian and the old coach were saying their goodbyes, Marcus was writing down his assignment back in his apartment. At first, he wrote that his passion was football and his goal was to make it to the NFL. But when he thought more about it, he didn't know the real reason he wanted to become a pro besides everyone always telling him since he was in high school that he was destined to be an NFL player. Late into the night, Marcus followed Brian's instructions and questioned what he really wanted and why. Just as he was falling asleep, some deeper ideas came to him. He turned on the light to scribble them on the paper on his nightstand, and satisfied he had found the answer, he went to sleep.

10

The Golden Rule

After the Trackside Diner, Brian headed home for a nice evening with Kelly and the kids. He took his new job description to heart and talked with Kelly about what she wanted from her career and their family, and he thought about how he could be more helpful to get her there. Reflecting on the story the old coach had told him about the professor and his students, he realized Kelly and the girls were his "coffee." Brian spent some time after they went to sleep jotting down a few notes in the golden notebook that the old coach had given him. One note in particular struck him with some inspiration. In the notebook, under the job description of a coach, he also wrote the words *Target* and *Direction*. With that, he fell asleep excited about the workout the old coach had in store for him.

4:30 a.m. is a lonely but quiet hour on the campus of a university. Brian actually now liked being an "early bird" since he felt he was able to be more productive and get an edge on the rest of the world that was still asleep. Although he really enjoyed working out, it had been a few years since he had given up on his consistent routine of running and lifting. With the lack of time from work and the arrival of his children, Brian couldn't remember when his last workout was, but he realized as he walked out to the practice field in the dark that it had been a long time. Brian found the old coach waiting for him by the gate.

"Wakey, wakey," he greeted Brian. "Good morning, and thanks for joining me out here. Even though I don't get to train as much as I would like anymore, this morning reminds me how I love to get in my workouts outside."

"From the look of you, Coach," said Brian as he admired the fact the old coach was lean and still had a frame shaped with solid muscle, "seems like you still have some life left in those arms and legs."

"Yeah, well, as you're going to learn today, sonny, it's not about me," replied the old coach with a smile. "Today we're going to learn a little bit more about you and you are going to learn the secret to carrying out your job description. So are you ready?"

"I guess as ready as I'll ever be," said Brian.

"Don't guess, kid," said the old coach as he bowed down to pass under the chain at the entrance of the practice field.

"You know that's why we have gates, right?" joked Brian.

"Just a habit," said the old coach. "As you will learn, your postures have a lot to do with who you are. That little act of bowing to the field is one of the ways I learned a long time ago to show respect for the place you train."

Brian didn't have a comeback for that statement and briefly tried to imagine all the places the old coach had been. Brian kept realizing in the time he had spent with him that the man spoke with a confidence borne of experience. His manner and calmness were something Brian hoped he could someday emulate.

"So are we ready for the workout?" asked Brian.

"Are you ready for another quick story first?" answered the old coach. "I want to tell you this one before you take what I am about to do to you the wrong way."

Something in the way he said "what I am about to do to you" made Brian nervous, but he just nodded in agreement.

"When I was much younger," began the old man, "I spent a period of my life searching for answers.

This search took me on a number of adventures around the world. At the time, I was looking for training and technical answers that could make me a more valuable coach. What I realize now is I was on a path trying to discover mastery. My travels took me to Japan, Brazil, Russia, Thailand, and many other countries, and eventually I found myself in Holland training at the top Dutch kickboxing school. Now if you know anything about the Dutch, they are the tallest population per capita in the world. So, needless to say, these guys I was training with were not only skilled, they were also *big*! I had been accepted into the school to do some training, and the head coach really impressed me. He was calm and cool, and really spent time teaching the finer points of technique. He also never missed a chance to teach a lesson."

"Sounds like someone I know," said Brian.

"Yeah," he said with a laugh. "Well, I was a few weeks into the training and up to that point had only been working on hitting bags and shadow boxing to refine my technique according to the Dutch style. But on this day, we were going to have some contact. The coach called it a 1-2 drill. What he did was partner up fighters and give them either the number 1 or 2. I was partnered with a huge Dutch fighter with almost 20 professional wins! To say it was intimidating was an understatement. To say it was scary was the truth … especially when the coach gave the instructions for the drill. Since the Dutch pride themselves on their ability to absorb punishment, this drill was designed to learn how to take punches and kicks. Obviously from my lack of experience and the size of my partner, I was not excited. The rules of the drill were simple. If the coach called the number 1 and your number was 1, you either hit or kicked your partner as hard as you could and he had to just take it. And if he called number 2, and your partner was number 2, your partner did the hitting and you did the receiving."

"That doesn't sound very fun at all," said Brian, getting a little more nervous about what the old coach might have planned for him.

"Well, I was number 1 and when he called my number, what do you think I did?"

"Follow the instructions?" asked Brian.

"No way!" laughed the old coach. "The guy was almost 7 feet tall! I punched him really lightly in the stomach and I think I remember asking if that was okay with a 'sir' at the end of the question!"

"Good move," said Brian.

"Not exactly, kid," said the old coach. "And that's the point of the story. When the coach saw this, he stopped the class and brought everyone in for a lesson. Without ever singling me out, he said something I'll never forget. He said, 'If you think you're being someone's friend by going easy on them right now, you are sadly mistaken. You are actually being their worst enemy! Many of these fighters will be in a ring soon with someone else giving them their best, and unless you do the same, they will not be prepared. So going gently sometimes is not the way to be someone's friend. Is that understood?' And with that he finally made eye contact with me and gave me a little wink letting me know who it was directed to."

"And then what did you do?" asked Brian.

"What?! I hit that guy as hard as I could!" the old coach said, laughing. "But I wanted to tell you that story to let you know why I have been challenging you these last few days and also to apologize in advance for what is about to happen now."

Because the old coach said this with a serious face, Brian knew things were about to get difficult. And he was right.

When the workout began, the old coach's calm and friendly demeanor completely changed. His tone became authoritative and harsh as he got Brian to line up on the 20-yard line. Then he started Brian on body squats and walking lunges, but no matter what Brian did, the old coach was in his face letting him know he was doing them wrong. And when Brian did things wrong, the coach prescribed a dose of either push-ups or burpees. Fifteen minutes into the workout, Brian was not only out of energy, he was also getting angry as well. The old coach was letting him have it, ranting about his lack of conditioning and his spare tire. Right as Brian was about to break, the old coach changed back to the man Brian had spent the last few days with.

"How did you like that?" asked the old coach.

"I didn't really like that or you right now," answered Brian, bent over in half through labored breathing.

"Well, what didn't you like about it in particular?" asked the old coach.

"I didn't like the way I was being punished," answered Brian as he continued to huff and puff. "I mean, I didn't exactly understand how you wanted me to do the exercises. And the negative stuff about my body wasn't exactly enjoyable, either."

"Well, how do you think your players like it when you use that style?" asked the old coach. "No one likes to be unsure of what they have to do and then criticized publicly when they don't do it. And if there was the rare individual who responds to some negative reinforcement, even he or she probably doesn't like personal attacks. Now understanding what I taught you about coaching, do you think those are the ways to complete your job description?"

"No, you're right," said Brian. "Over the years, my workouts and coaching have gotten tougher, but I guess the kids really haven't. And the further I got from working out, the less respect I gave to how tough those exercises were both physically and mentally. Like your story, I was being their worst enemy instead of giving them the things they really needed."

"Like I keep telling you," said the old coach, "don't beat yourself up about past things you didn't know. Once you learn coaching is more about encouragement than intimidation, it isn't going to happen again."

Brian, who had by now caught his breath, but also realized he wasn't in the shape he needed to be, said, "I hope that secret doesn't involve any more burpees!"

"Ha!" laughed the old man. "Anyone can make you tired, kid. That isn't a secret. That is actually easy. The secret I have for you is more difficult. It's about making someone their best."

"Well, before the sun comes up and I have to go," said Brian, "What's the secret?"

"I call it the Golden Rule of coaching. Once I discovered this, it made carrying out my job description of coaching much easier," said the old coach.

"Golden Rule?" asked Brian. "You mean like the 'do unto others' rule?"

"No," said the old coach. "Not that Golden Rule. And anyway, once you understand my Golden Rule, you'll see why the one you've been taught doesn't work well anyway. So here it is. My Golden Rule of coaching is *You have to be more enthusiastic about someone other than yourself.*"

"I like it," said Brian. "Makes sense, but why did you say the original Golden Rule doesn't work well?"

"The original," said the old coach, "doesn't point the enthusiasm or concern in the right direction for a coach. You see, 'do unto others as you would have them to do unto you' has you more concerned about how you want to be treated. What I have learned from being a coach is that it's all about understanding how they want to be treated. What you may like or want could be totally different than what they want."

"I never thought of it that way," admitted Brian. "So are you saying a coach has to be more focused on others than himself?"

"That is exactly the job of a coach," said the old coach. "And what my Golden Rule does is remind you to focus on what other people want WITH ENTHU-SIASM. Think about it, who doesn't want someone out there to be excited about and fired up about them and their dreams?"

"Again, it makes sense, Coach," said Brian. "Why haven't I realized this sooner?"

"Simple. Because you've been more worried about what *you* are enthusiastic about. You've been worrying about getting your own riches instead of realizing the way to get them is by enriching the lives of others. You have to think of your enthusiasm, or lack of it, as being contagious. Because my friend, it is. So, make sure you are infecting your athletes the right way."

"I really like this," said Brian. "So to make sure I'm getting the right clarity, are you saying my job is to take people where they want to go that they can't get to them-selves, and the best way to do it is to be more enthusiastic about them than myself?"

"By Jove, I think he's got it, Watson!" joked the old coach.

With his breathing back to normal and the sweat finally starting to evaporate, Brian remembered that shortly before this lesson, the old coach was kicking his butt with punishing exercises.

"So to be my athletes' friend," asked Brian, "Am I supposed to just go easier on them in the training?"

"No," said the old coach, "that isn't the point at all. Just remember that the goal isn't to just make your athletes tired. Remember that the goal of every moment a coach spends with an athlete should be focused on making them better. Sometimes that will involve really tough training, too. Tough love from a coach still has its place because you aren't just getting them ready for the battle on the field. You also get them ready for the battle called life. So don't worry, kid, you will still get to wear them out sometimes. You just have to be sure to fill one tank when you are emptying the other."

"Fill tanks?" asked Brian. "What does that mean?"

"Most coaches only think about the physical tank with their athletes," said the old coach. "I know because I started my career the same way. I was the king of killer workouts and wouldn't let my athletes out of a session without breaking them down and emptying that tank. In fact, my athletes had a nickname for me about it."

"Wow," said Brian. "I know what you mean. I've heard the nickname they have for me too for the exact same reason."

"Don't take it as a compliment, kid," said the old coach. "Being known for hammering people with workouts is nothing to be proud of. Coaches like that have forgotten the real purpose of training."

"The real purpose?" repeated Brian.

"Yes. The real purpose for any training session is not to be or act tough. It's not to show how creative you can be, either. Any coach can stretch someone's legs. The sole purpose of training should be to stretch their limits to get a result that gets someone closer to where they want to go."

"When you put it that way, Coach, I guess I've forgotten that purpose along the way, too. I've been on a power trip, trying to show these kids I'm tough."

"That's why I'm here," said the old coach. "To show you that you don't have to be tough to get results. Yes, you are going to have to empty an athlete's physical tank from time to time to produce results, but the second tank is the one that most coaches have seemed to have forgotten about."

"And what tank is that?" asked Brian.

"The emotional tank," said the old coach. "As you are emptying the physical tank with workouts filled with drills and exercises, a great coach is simultaneously filling the emotional tank of an athlete to keep them focused and motivated when the going gets tough. Exercise that just empties the physical tank is something an athlete tries to get *through*. Workouts that also fill the emotional tank are ones athletes and coaches get *from*."

"I could sure use some advice in that area," said Brian. "Most of my workouts are just about counting reps and sets."

"With my two favorite tricks to fill the emotional tank," said the old coach, "You will learn how to make those reps and sets count. When you start focusing on building more than strong biceps, that's when you start building stronger relationships."

"Well, I am all ears, Coach," said Brian with some newfound enthusiasm.

"That's just it, Bri," said the old coach. "One of the tricks will require the ears, but to really fill the emotional tank, you will be required to either learn to properly use your hands or feet, too."

"What do you mean?" asked Brian.

"I mean that the best way to connect with your athletes is by delivering feedback that is a combination of what you say and how you physically navigate what I call 'the crucial distance.'"

"Okay, Coach, you've lost me again," said Brian. "You're gonna have to explain that one."

"Gladly, son," said the old coach. "These next few ideas might be some of the most important I can share to help you. In fact, until you understand and begin to practice and use these skills, you will have no chance at being the best coach in the world. And the first one starts with just five words. In fact, I call them the five most powerful words a coach can ever say to someone." The old coach paused for dramatic effect.

"They are simple, yet so profound. Easy to say, yet rarely do we say them to the people closest to us. They are so effective, but we often keep them to ourselves even when they are true," said the old coach.

"Those five words are I AM PROUD OF YOU."

"That's it?" asked Brian.

"That's it?" repeated the old coach, sounding annoyed. "Tell me, how often are you using that little gem? And not just after a kid makes a play on the field. Let me know how you are using that with your wife and kids when they do something that you are actually proud of."

Brian again put his head down and kicked at the turf.

"Exactly," said the old man. "Coaches like you are so caught up in telling everyone what they are doing wrong that you have lost the ability to recognize and appreciate when someone is doing something right. And even when you do notice, it's like pulling teeth to get you to say something about it. Like if you share some good news there will be less goodness left for someone else. Well, I am here to let you know it isn't true. When you use those five words in the right way and authentically, it can become your greatest creator of both relationships and results. As a coach, you should strive to never miss an opportunity to say, 'I am proud of you.'"

"You've got me again, Coach," said Brian. "I guess since I didn't hear it much when I was a kid, maybe I'm just repeating the cycle. You're right about one thing: I haven't probably said that to my kids in years and maybe never to Kelly. Do I just start saying it over and over? I don't want it to lose its effectiveness by overdoing it."

"The key," the old coach said, "is to be on the lookout for good things and when you see them, let the person know about it. I am not telling you to say it for every little thing, but I can assure you that if your athletes and family got just one that they deserved a day, it would make a big difference. Heck, one workout a week is better than none, isn't it?"

"Yeah, I guess you're right," said Brian.

"Stop guessing!" snapped the old man. "You know it's right. So stop being like everyone else when it comes to hearing the truth about something. Instead of thinking about all the reasons it might not work, I want you to give it a shot and think about some ways that it can. That is the only way you will know anyhow. Like I learned from a tough guy I knew long ago, 'You won't know if you don't throw!'"

"Okay, Coach," said Brian sheepishly, "I got it. I'll set my radar for positive things and do my best to use the five words."

"Good," said the old coach more calmly. "And make sure you do it today. The key with any new skill is to strike while the iron is hot. Don't wait around until it grows cold. Now that I've beat that horse, next is to understand how to make those five words even more powerful. And all you have to do is be able to properly navigate about one foot of distance."

"On the gridiron, I've had to learn to navigate over a hundred yards," said Brian. "I think I can do one foot for sure."

"Don't answer too fast, sparky," said the old coach. "It took me a couple of decades to get it right. Remember, everything I am teaching you is going to take hard work and practice. Just like you are learning training is not the same as coaching, knowing is not the same as doing."

"I understand, Coach," said Brian, really meaning it, too.

"Okay, so now let's work on your navigation skills," said the old coach. "The foot of distance I am talking about is the section of a person's back between the shoulders and butt. If you want to be a great coach, you have to know when a person needs a pat on the back and when they need a kick in the pants. Understanding your athlete and properly navigating the distance is critical to getting the result you want."

"I love that one," laughed Brian. "And I think I get it, too. I've had some athletes who really needed that pat and some who needed me to get them angry to play at their best. But I never seemed to get it right. Sometimes I would just get lucky."

"Luck has nothing to do with it," answered the old coach. "Let that be used for how the ball bounces, but never think of luck as a strategy."

"So do you have some navigation strategies for me then?"

"Absolutely," smiled the old coach. "Lighting a fire under someone is always easier than lighting a fire inside of them. Since you already seem to be pretty good at coaching with veins in your neck, let's focus on how to coach with a pat on the back. And the first one is not only way easier than the five most powerful words, but when you also use this strategy with those words, the effect is greatly multiplied. So let me ask you: How is your high five?"

"What do you mean?" asked Brian.

"I mean," said the old coach, "Are you great at throwing a high five? You know when you have had a good high five with someone. There's a connection ... an energy that's created. It's a way of using contact to accentuate a job well done. So again, I ask you. How is your high five? Is it so great that your players will run through a brick wall to get one?"

"To be honest again, Coach," said Brian, "I can't say my high five is that great. In fact, I'm not the rah-rah guy throwing them around much."

"Rah-rah guy?!" exclaimed the old coach, showing a flash of temper again. "Let me tell you this. If you think giving a high five is rah-rah, and you are somehow hinting that it's negative, take a look in the mirror, pal. That just means *you're* negative. Everyone likes a high five. Anyone who says different is either negative, lazy, or hasn't learned to be enthusiastic about someone else yet. The high five is the personification of the Golden Rule. And again, before you start thinking of reasons not to do it, I am daring you to give it a shot and see."

"Sorry for firing you up again," Brian said. "You're right about that ... and that I've been negative. I'm just making excuses. I agree I need to dish out some more high fives. I can really improve there. Funny to say this, but do you have any advice for a good high five?"

"Think of the high five as just an example," said the old coach, regaining his calm. "You could use a fist bump, a pat on the back, or even a special handshake. I once knew a coach who had a different one for each one of his athletes. And you know what? They would work their butts off to get one of those shakes. The key is that you're looking for positive behaviors and you use your words and contacts to reward them for it. After all, every great coach knows what gets rewarded gets repeated."

Realizing he had to get ready for the workday, Brian and the old coach made their way back outside the gate. The old coach bowed down under the chain again and this time Brian followed suit. Because of that action, the old coach raised his hand and said, "Good job, kid, your old coach is proud of you," and Brian reflexively gave him a solid high five.

"See you at Trackside tonight?" Brian asked as he opened his car door.

"You can count on it," said the old coach as he walked away.

Brian immediately felt the power of the combination of the Golden Rule, the five most powerful words, and a high five. As he got in his car, he realized the golden color of the notebook was the perfect reminder for what he had learned that day. He opened the book and took some notes:

A coach's Golden Rule: You have to be more enthusiastic about someone else than yourself.

The five most powerful words a coach can say: "I am proud of you."

Closing his notebook, Brian realized how important and necessary the information was that the old coach was sharing. As he started his car, he promised himself he would use his new coaching skills that day both on the field and at home.

11

A Turning Point

Brian got a quick shower and made it in time for the team meetings. The conversations revolved around the game against the big in-state rivals on the upcoming Saturday. Since the other team was currently a Top 25 program, Brian's school was not only not expected to win, but there was added pressure from the previous evening about the disrespect shown to their school as a result of some students vandalizing a famous statue on campus. Although the painting of the other school's founder's statue in rival team colors had become a thing of tradition, it still stirred up anger when some enterprising students were able to pull it off. Coach Olsen was using this "blatant disrespect for our school" as motivation for both the staff and the team because he knew what a victory on Saturday could mean for the program. It had been five years since their last victory against that team, and their fan base, alumni, and administration were starting to lose faith. Coach Olsen was looking for all the ammunition he could get.

Just like the previous day, Brian found Marcus in the locker room getting ready for practice. This time, Marcus's body language told Brian he was a little more excited to see him. It also gave Brian a clue that Marcus had taken his homework assignment seriously. Brian asked Marcus if they could chat again in the film room before practice. Marcus was ready and they both went inside and had a seat in the same chairs.

"Marcus," said Brian, "I have a feeling you spent some time on your homework last night."

"Yes, sir," replied Marcus pulling out his paper and unfolding it, "It actually took me a lot longer to come up with my answers than I thought it would."

"I know what you mean," said Brian, looking with a sense of pride at the paper covered in a number of ideas that had obviously been written and crossed out in an attempt to find just the right words. "When I tried to answer the same thing, I realized I hadn't spent much time ever thinking about what it was I wanted or what drove me to want it in the first place."

"Same," said Marcus. "No one has really asked what I thought before. I've just been told by a lot of people what I should want. But instead of just listing those ideas, I kept digging and I did like you said. As I looked at each answer I gave, I forced myself to go deeper. And that's when I realized the real reason I want my goal. And it also helped me to understand the bad stuff I've been thinking about lately."

"What do you mean?" asked Brian.

"At first, I instinctively wrote down that my passion is football and my goal was to make it to the NFL. But then I realized that since I had always been so good when I was young, that's what people always told me that I wanted. People like my mom and my close friends. Instead of just going along with their dreams for me, instead I dug deeper. I asked myself what I really wanted and why I wanted it. Yeah, football has a lot to do with my identity of how I think about myself and how other people think about me, but I found out that I had a bigger passion than just football. I have a passion to be great at something. So yeah, it is football right now, but someday, no matter how far I go, football will be over. If I didn't have a bigger passion, that could be a big problem, like I've seen for other players who do some bad things once their career is over. So, my passion is greatness. Right now, the way I am pursuing that is with football. But my big reason why I'm chasing greatness is different than I originally thought, too." Marcus paused for a moment, then continued.

"Like some of the guys on the team, the goal is to make the NFL. But when I wrote that down, something was missing. Yeah, that's something I want, but there are only fifteen hundred jobs in the league and they're currently taken. And the eighty thousand people who sit in the stands at a game would love to be in the NFL, too. Just wanting to make it or make money isn't enough. I asked the hard question last night of why I will do what it takes to make an NFL squad. I looked past the money and fame and figured out my real purpose behind making the league. I want to thank you because this reminder already has me refocused."

"This is great stuff, Marcus," said Brian. "I am really proud of you," he said with a smile and gave him a fist bump. "You've gone beyond what I would have expected a kid your age to come up with here. And you are absolutely right about the league. There has to be more than money driving you. I have seen players forget that. That's why I say NFL stands for Not For Long. So ... what was the thing you found that got you refocused?"

"My family," answered Marcus. "I don't think you know much about them, do you, Coach?"

"Well, no, Marcus," replied Brian. "I know I've met a number of other family members of players on the team, but I haven't had the privilege to meet yours yet, and we haven't really ever talked about them."

"That's just it," said Marcus. "My family hasn't gotten a chance to see me play in college, at least in person. And not just because they live so far away and they don't have the money to travel. It's some stuff I haven't shared before, but last night gave me the idea that I should. You see, my father was killed when I was young and it was up to my mother to raise me and my little sister in the murder capital of our state. The place is still a mess and I worry about them a lot. They'll never get out of there unless I make something of myself. Last night I found out they are my purpose. If I make the league in football, I'll have the money to get them out and keep them safe. And to be honest, I think until this exercise, I'd forgotten about that. My first few years here at school have been a letdown and not just for me, but for them, too. I guess that's why I've been thinking bad things lately."

"What kind of bad things are you talking about, Marcus?" asked Brian with concern.

That's when Marcus did something Brian would not have expected. But even at 6′3″ and 235 pounds of muscle, everyone has a heart. Marcus put his head down in embarrassment and started to cry.

"I'm not deaf to what people say, man. With all the talk that I haven't reached my potential over the last couple years, I started to believe the league would be impossible. So I started thinking about giving up. I've never quit anything in my life, but with the pressure to perform and feeling like I'm on my own, I was starting to look for a way out. I don't know. I guess sometimes I just wished someone would blow out my knee or give me a concussion, so I could just quit and no one would blame me. And after you ripping me in front of the team, I thought I finally had reason to do it. When I walked off that field at practice, I really thought it was the last time I was ever going to be on the field. I saw how alone I was and no one seemed to care or be on my side. But when I got home, I really didn't want it to be over, but I didn't know what to do. I started to panic, and then I got your text. If you didn't send that text, I don't know where I would be right now."

Brian was touched and saddened by not only Marcus's honesty, but also by understanding both his pressure to perform and his feeling of solitude. He also realized he had a lot of blame in why his player was feeling so down. He put his arm around Marcus and tears started to well up in his eyes, too.

"I'm sorry for laying that on you," said Marcus.

"You're not the one who should feel sorry," replied Brian. "It should be me. There are so many ways I haven't been a good coach for you. And that's because I didn't understand what it really means to be a coach. I haven't found out what drives you until now, and I definitely haven't given you the tools or skills to take you where you want to go. I never gave you the time you deserved and as a result have done the opposite of what a good coach should do. You have nothing to be ashamed of. But I want to thank you for sharing your story with me. Now I have clarity on what you want and I am making you a solemn promise to do my best to help you get there. You have two seasons left and I swear if you give me another chance, I will give you all I've got. You have too much talent not to."

"Thanks," said Marcus, wiping his eyes. "I'd like that. And again I wanna apologize for getting upset. That isn't usually my style."

"No apologies, Marcus," said Brian. "You showed me more courage right there than you know, and if you let me coach you, you are doing me the biggest favor. I'm getting the second chance, not you."

"No, Coach," said Marcus. "Because of your text and that exercise last night, I'm getting a second chance at this thing, too. Now that I remember why I'm in it to win it, I'll work even harder."

"Harder is only one part of the equation for being a great linebacker. You'll have to work smarter, too. And you're not the only one who's been reminded of who he used to be. Back in my day, I was given a secret that I think just might help us both do something big on the field."

"What secret is that?" asked Marcus, now more composed.

"I can't tell you yet," replied Brian with a smile. "That's why they call it a secret, kid. And hey, crying isn't exactly my style, either. What do you say we make sure no one finds out about it? Like my wife and kids?"

"This is one secret that's safe with me," said Marcus.

This short meeting brought Brian and Marcus closer as a coach and athlete. At the end of their talk, they discussed the upcoming game and Brian asked if Marcus could meet him tomorrow at the same time before practice to go over the secret he had to show him.

12

The Two Abilities

After another solid practice with the team, Brian was excited to get to the diner to meet with the old coach and report how everything had been going. He was using what the old coach had shown him and was already seeing and feeling the results. In particular, he noticed that the high fives were becoming contagious with his linebacking crew, and when he let one of the players know he was proud of him for his effort, the player gave even more.

When Brian pulled up at Trackside, he could already see the old coach waiting for him at their usual table.

"How's it going?" asked the old coach. "I may not know much, but I do feel I'm a good interpreter of body language. And from your energy, I have a feeling you have some good news for me today."

"You read me right as usual, Coach," said Brian. "But I think I have both good and bad news for you today."

After saying this, Brian sat down and after ordering a different salad and water, he started back in on the conversation.

"For the good news," Brian said, "I believe that I made some big progress with Marcus today. The paper exercise was a real home run and he took it much more seriously than I expected. Actually, the kid surprised me with his answers."

"I told you he might be more than you think," said the old coach with a smile.

"And not only has his effort increased," continued Brian, "but that effort and the connection we are demonstrating is rubbing off on the rest of the team."

"How so?" asked the old coach.

"Well, you were right. It's all about what I am calling the 'coaching combination' you showed me. The Golden

Rule, high fives and five most powerful words are working. Now the other players are high-fiving and I swear I could see them getting a little more excited for each other when they did something good. Maybe rah-rah is a little more magical than I thought."

"It isn't magic," said the old coach, "just because you can't see it. You believe in electricity, don't you?"

"Sure," replied Brian.

"How about gravity?" asked the old coach.

"Come on. Yeah, gravity, too," said Brian with a smile.

"Well, enthusiasm works a lot like both of those. Electricity carries a powerful charge to create illumination and gravity has an ability to pull things together. I believe enthusiasm does the same thing. When you are enthusiastic about someone else, you can light them up, and great energy and enthusiasm will always draw more people to you. So, enthusiasm, just like electricity and gravity, is a real thing that you just can't see."

"I'll agree with that," said Brian. "And just like electricity and gravity can be invisible, I can see the results of what they produce. And in the case of the team and Marcus right now, the Golden Rule is producing a positive result."

"I like it, kid," said the old coach. "And I like that you gave my idea the name of the 'coaching combination.' I'm also proud of you for applying the concepts of it so quickly. So, now that we have the good news out of the way, what's the bad news that you have to share?"

"Well," answered Brian, "the meeting with Marcus got really emotional to say the least. He opened up to me not only about his passion and purpose, but also about his family and the stress that it's put him under. I really feel bad for the kid."

"Is that the bad news?" asked the old coach.

"No," replied Brian, "the bad news is his answers really hammered home that I am not that great of a coach. It forced me to realize that I haven't fulfilled my job as a coach and I have actually let him down. Even though I know it was good for him to open up and flush out those feelings, it really left me feeling like a bit of a failure. I wish I could go back in time and know this stuff earlier."

"Hindsight, as you know, is 20/20. I understand learning new things can make you aware of the things you didn't know or do, but that's just how life works. Life is just one big practice session where you should always be looking to learn new things and get better. Like I've heard, the best day to plant a tree is 20 years ago and the second best day to plant one is today. You can't change the past, so I wouldn't waste too much of your time there, kid. As you will learn when you get as old as me, time is the most important resource you've got."

"I get it," said Brian. "I just see now how many mistakes I've been making."

"Mistakes are part of the game, kid," said the old coach. "And learning from your mistakes is the way you get better. I want you to remember, no one is perfect. You're gonna make mistakes. Heck, look at other sports, for example. If you get a hit three out of ten times in baseball or make three out of ten three-pointers in basketball for your career, they might call you a hall-of-famer! And look at football. With a hundred plays per game, if a defensive player just got a sack out of one of them each game of his career, he could be a superstar, too! That's failing 99 percent of the time. Now don't get me wrong.

I'm not saying to set your percentages low, but you gotta be okay with making the occasional mistake and growing from it."

"I hear you," said Brian. "I've heard Coach Olsen refer to it as failing forward."

"Exactly. And when you do it right, you shouldn't get upset. It isn't bad news, Brian, it's the best news because you can see what you have become. In just a few days, you have already grown a lot as a coach. And in particular, I want you to know I have seen you improve on the two most important abilities you could have as a coach."

"Sounds like there's another lesson in there," said Brian with a smile. "So now that I understand the coaching combination, what are the two most important coaching abilities?"

"Shouldn't you have your pen and notebook with you?" asked the old coach.

"Got it right here, Coach," Brian said, pulling the small golden book out of his front pocket. "And I've been adding some things of my own in there, too."

"Nice work," said the old coach. "You actually having that book has to do with the first ability. It's interesting how many coaches, once they officially become a coach, forget it."

"Forget the book?"

"No," said the old coach. "They forget how to be coachable! The first major ability of a coach is *coachability*. I define 'coachability' as when you learn something new that is the right thing to do and you do it. It seems unfortunate that once people become a coach, they feel they can no longer admit that they don't know everything. Then, instead of trying to continue to pursue new information and try new things, they get stuck in their ways."

"Man," said Brian, "When you put it that way, I know a lot of coaches like that."

"Me, too," said the old coach. "And I happened to be one of them. All of a sudden, when I became an authority, I lost my curiosity. And when I lost that, I stopped being a student. And I started becoming a dinosaur."

"You know dinosaurs are extinct, right?" Brian joked.

"No, they aren't. There are dinosaurs all over the place. What I mean is when you stop upgrading and adapting to new changes or information you become known as a dinosaur. After you become one for long enough, then you become extinct. So, there are dinosaurs in every field today hanging on."

"I feel you on that," said Brian. "I hope I haven't been a fossil for too long yet."

"No," said the old coach, "you're already developing your coachability again. You're not only learning new information, but you're also applying it. Yes, part of being coachable is getting your curiosity back for new ideas, but you also have to know the difference between being an information gatherer and an action taker. Knowing what to do is useless if you never do what you know."

"You're right," said Brian. "And I'm glad to be a student again. On the football field and in the classroom, I was a student for a long time before I ever got to be the teacher. But now that I'm the teacher doesn't mean I should stop learning."

"See," said the old coach with a grin, "there you go being coachable again. You're right, a coach must constantly invest time and energy to improve as a coach. And don't forget that goes for being a husband and father, too."

"Got any tips in that department, Coach?" asked Brian.

"The best advice I could give is something I learned a long time ago the hard way," said the old coach sadly. "The best thing you can do in front of your kids is love your wife."

Brian paused to absorb that nugget of wisdom from the coach and then wrote down the word *Coachability* and the definition that the old coach had told him in his notebook. He wrote Kelly's and the girls' names next to it, too.

"You said you've seen me improving on two important coaching abilities. What's the other one?" asked Brian.

"The second ability is another one that most coaches wouldn't guess. But as you've already learned this week both on the field and at home, it could be the most important if you're ever going to carry out the Golden Rule. In our day and age of constant distraction, this is the one ability that is disappearing from coaching at an alarming rate. Do you have any ideas what I'm talking about?"

"I think I know where you're going with this, Coach," said Brian. "Let's see if my coachability is as good as you say. As I've been reviewing what you taught me and what I've been using to see improvement of the people around me, I'm guessing it has something to do with attention?"

"Number one, stop guessing already! And number two, you are really close. The second ability actually has to do with what you need to have in order to pay that attention. The second ability of a great coach is availability. Just like a player who isn't available to play in the game can never make an impact, a coach who is never available for his or her athletes can never make a difference. As you are learning this week, when you make yourself available to a person, that time and attention is reciprocated with results."

"I have to hand it to you," said Brian, "You have a way of making this all so simple. Why didn't I get this lesson in school?"

"Stop worrying about the past," said the old coach. "Be glad you're getting the lesson now. Better to spend your energy on what you have left than what you have lost, kid. In order for your athletes to ever make their minds and bodies available to you, you are going to have to be available for them first!"

"Got it," said Brian, as he wrote down the word *Availability* in his golden notebook and jotted down a few ideas about that important coaching ability.

"So tell me," said the old coach, "What was it that Marcus wrote on his enthusIASM paper that was so surprising?"

"I knew he came from a single-parent family and from a tough area," said Brian. "But a lot of players I've coached have had similar situations. I didn't know the whole story, though. His father was killed when he was young and his mother and sister live in one of the crime-ridden cities in the South. He's putting a lot of pressure on himself to make it to the NFL to get them out of there. With his play the way it's been, he feels he's really let everyone down. But the part that really made me nervous was the way that he said he had almost been wishing for an injury and then he mentioned he 'didn't know where he would be right now' if I hadn't written him that text you suggested. I don't really know if he meant giving up on football or giving up on life. Man, I'm glad you told me to send that text, Coach, because I was so stubborn I know I wouldn't have done it otherwise."

"You have learned another invaluable lesson here, Brian. And also a reminder about a story you have already told me."

"What story?" asked Brian.

"The story about when your soccer coach called you Chubby," said the old coach. "Remember that?"

"How could I forget," replied Brian.

"Just like that story, you have to be reminded that as a coach, you never know who you're talking to. I mean, you might know who they are, but you don't know what they're going through or what they're thinking at the time. Because a coach should be aware of this, a coach should always make sure that the goal of any interaction is to leave the person better than before you met them."

"I think I often forget that one," said Brian as he made another note in his notebook. "Do you have any tips for making sure I don't forget in the future?"

"That's easy," said the old coach. "All you need to do is use an idea a mentor of mine had from long ago."

"Is this back with the dinosaurs?" Brian asked with a laugh.

"Come on, kid, I am not that old," said the old man.

"Sorry," said Brian. "I couldn't resist. Please continue with the coaching."

"Okay," said the old coach. "When I was coming up as a coach, I spent a lot of time following around a coach who I considered an amazing success. To me, as a younger coach, when I saw he had produced a number of past state champion athletes and even some national champs, I wanted results like that, too. So I asked him one day how he had had so much success, and he laughed in my face. He said, 'Success? I've been coaching for over 30 years and out of thousands of athletes, that handful were my only champs!' But then that coach gave me one of his coaching secrets that changed me forever. He told me, 'Yes, I had a few diamonds over my career as a coach. But I never knew which one of those thousands of athletes it was going to be. So instead of helping the ones I thought might be the best, I decided to polish all of them. This ensured that any time I was with anyone, I would be sure to do my best to understand them and say something that would make them better than before I met them.'"

"Thank you for that," said Brian as he drew the shape of a diamond in his notebook and made a few notes.

"The way you can thank me," said the old coach, "is not by telling me about it, but by doing it."

"Will do," replied Brian. "And thanks for all your availability, too. The idea about making mistakes has taken a little of the pressure off me, too."

"Pressure isn't always a bad thing," said the old coach. "It shows you want to get better. Remember, it takes pressure to make a diamond. No pressure, no diamonds."

Brian and the old coach finished their meals and even discussed a little strategy for the upcoming game. Brian really valued the time the old coach was spending with him and promised himself he would become more available not only to his players, but also to his wife and kids. He also entertained the idea of mentoring a young coach when he was older, too. The two men said their goodbyes and agreed to meet for another early morning workout the next day.

In the car, Brian found himself more excited than usual to get home. Knowing it was not only acceptable but also important to leave work at the doorstep gave him a newfound sense of power. When he walked in the door, he took the old coach's advice and greeted his wife with a hug and a kiss.

"Ewwwww," cried Jenny when she saw her dad's display of affection. "Jaime! Come quick! Daddy is kissing Mommy!"

Jaime came running from her room. To make sure she didn't miss out on the show, Brian gave Kelly another kiss, to the delight of the kids. By the way the kids were reacting with big smiles, Brian saw the old coach had been right again. He realized he hadn't been showing enough affection around the house, too.

"Wherever you've been stopping off on the way home," said Kelly with a smile, "I guess it's okay you're a little later than usual when I get a welcome like that!"

"Sorry I'm late, Kell," said Brian with a wink. "As you probably see, I'm learning some stuff with the old coach that has me energized."

His wife and children watched in surprise as Brian took out his phone and turned it off, setting it on a nearby table. This small action had a tremendous effect. At dinner, Brian asked about Kelly's day at work and the kids' day at school. Without the constant distractions and reminders that come with a vibrating phone in his pocket, Brian was able to pay attention and concentrate on their answers. Availability was even more powerful than Brian had imagined.

After dinner, Brian helped Kelly clear the table and load the dishwasher. He actually felt good about helping out for a change. Then the whole family sat down and watched an episode of *American Ninja Warrior*. The girls were so excited, they started jumping from the couch to the floor emulating the athletes on the screen. When little Jaime followed her big sister off the couch and stuck the landing, Brian cheered and gave her a big high five. Jenny followed suit and gave her little sister a high five, too. Showing how contagious and addictive a high five can be, Jaime ran over for a high five and a hug from Kelly, too.

After the girls brushed their teeth, Brian spent time in Jaime's room for her "back tickle," and then read with Jenny for a few minutes. Before turning out the lights in each of his daughter's rooms, Brian made sure to single out one good thing each of them had done that day and told them, "I am proud of you."

As they were getting ready for bed, Kelly asked Brian about his day. He showed her the golden notebook and shared what he had been learning from the old coach. Brian made sure to ask questions about her day and really listen to her answers, too. As Brian drifted off to sleep, he realized the evening had been one of the most relaxing he had had in some time.

13

Pointing Fingers

The next morning, Brian got up, fixed himself a healthy (and smaller) breakfast of oatmeal and eggs, and made his way again to the practice field before the sun came up. He could feel his legs and lower back were already getting sore from the quick workout on the previous day. No stranger to pain, he realized it had been awhile since he experienced the soreness of training. Even though he was moving a little gingerly, he also remembered the pride that came along with the pain of a workout. When he got out of his car, even though he was early for the scheduled workout, the old coach was again already there.

"Top of the morning," greeted the old coach.

"Good morning, Coach," replied Brian. "I don't know how you do it. Seems like you're always pumped up with energy."

"A person is always on fire when he does what he loves. And a long time ago, I figured out it wasn't who I was working with, I just loved coaching people and watching them improve. Ever since then, I've never had a problem getting up in the morning. The only trouble I ever had was that all that energy had a tendency of keeping me up late, too."

The old coach bent down again under the chain in front of the practice field entrance. This time Brian did as well and paid a little more attention to his movement and the reason behind why he was doing it.

"Spending time with you this week has helped me realize that, too," said Brian.

"Well, before we run out of time, let's get started with the workout. I have another lesson for you today and I promise not to beat you up this time. But this one is going to require you to listen. Got it?"

"I'm ready," said Brian. "Getting a couple workouts in a row and paying more attention to my diet has actually inspired me. I think you navigated the distance on my back correctly with that kick in the pants, Coach."

"Ha," laughed the old coach, "well, don't go thanking me too soon, because I have a few more kicks left for you today. Have you ever done a star jump?"

"Star jump?" asked Brian. "What's that?"

"Sorry," said the old coach, "maybe I'm showing my age again. You might know it as a jumping jack."

"Ohhh," said Brian, "yeah, I'm pretty familiar with those. We start the team out with them before practices and games."

"Great," said the old coach. "Then this should be a piece of cake. Okay, then I want you to give me ten good jumping jacks on my command. Ready and go!"

Brian started his jumping jacks and after he did his tenth repetition, he raised his hands halfway out to the sides and then put them back down. Then the old coach started in on him.

"You call those jumping jacks?" yelled the old coach. "Whatsamatter, can't you count to ten? I told you ten and you did ten and a half. I mean, I appreciate the extra effort and all, but give me a break. I thought you said you do these? You are killing me here, Knight!"

Brian, a little confused, blurted out, "But … "

"But!" interrupted the old coach. "If if's and but's were candy and nuts, we'd all have a Merry Christmas! And what about your arms? They were never straight and you didn't count out loud, either! Are you just here to make me look bad?"

Brian, still taken aback, was not sure what to think. The old coach took a few deep breaths and collected himself.

"Okay," said the old coach more calmly. "Sorry for yelling. I was using something simple and familiar to teach you the most important movement skill a coach has to know in order to be the best."

"It's okay," said Brian, relieved to see there would be a lesson in the old coach's manic behavior. "So you think the jumping jack is the most important movement skill to learn? Some people might argue it's the squat, deadlift, or bench press."

"No," said the old coach, "I was using the jumping jack as an opportunity to teach you the most important movement skill. And it doesn't involve weights or jumping around. All you need is just one finger."

"I hope this doesn't involve one-finger pushups," said Brian.

"No," laughed the old coach, "this movement is performed standing, my friend. So let me ask you, whose fault was it when you did the jumping jacks wrong?"

"It was my fault."

"Wrong!"

"But I did ten and a half when you only asked for ten," said Brian.

"Yes," answered the old coach, "but did I ever tell you how I wanted you to stop? Did I tell you exactly how I wanted the exercise to look? Was there any example or anything?"

"No," replied Brian, "I guess there wasn't."

"Then whose fault was it that you did it wrong?" asked the old coach.

"It was your fault?" asked Brian tentatively.

"Yes!" exclaimed the old coach. "It was completely my fault. So now let me show you the correct way to do a jumping jack."

The old coach then instructed Brian on exactly how he wanted the jumping jack to be performed. He had him start with his feet together and hands at his sides and let him know this was the bottom position of the exercise. Then showing him and then having Brian raise his arms completely with his arms straight and feet apart, he explained how this would be the top position. After going over where and how the feet should hit the ground, the old coach then performed ten perfect repetitions with a sharp and distinct finish at the end, emphasizing this was exactly how he wanted to see Brian perform it.

Then Brian performed ten perfect jumping jacks matching the instructions and demonstration the old coach had just given. They were much sharper and cleaner than his previous set.

When he finished, the old coach smiled at him, and Brian smiled back, knowing he had nailed it.

"Perfect!" said the old coach. "Now…who was responsible for you performing the exercise perfectly this time?"

"You were," said Brian.

"Noooooooo," yelled the old coach. "You are just like all the other coaches who don't know the movement skill I'm talking about! That perfect performance wasn't because of me, it was because of you! You were the one who did the work. That one was all you."

Brian just had the look of a confused student on his face.

"The movement skill I am talking about," said the old coach, "is knowing which way to point your finger when it is time to either *take the blame or accept the credit*. Most people are terrible at this and as a result, it causes a lot of problems. What I was trying to teach you with this exercise is that when something is going wrong on a coach's watch, he has to accept the blame. If someone is doing something wrong, the coach has to figure out what he could do better to make it right. If an athlete or a team isn't getting the desired result, the coach has to point at himself and see what he can do differently. But most people don't do it this way. Most people, unfortunately, are blame makers and credit takers. A great coach learns to point his finger differently to be a credit maker and a blame taker."

"That makes sense, Coach," said Brian. "But aren't there some times when a problem isn't the coach's fault? Like, for example, we've had an issue where some kids have been late to practice. I can't be expected to control traffic or the weather, can I?"

"Still your fault," replied the old coach. "If your athletes are late, or can't get to bed, or aren't eating right, there must be either something you can do or aren't doing that could make sure it doesn't happen. I know it's hard to accept this, but that is part of the job. You have to do everything in your power to make sure you get the result you want. And if you don't, you have to keep pointing the finger at yourself and take the blame until you do."

"Well, I know I haven't been doing that one right," said Brian. "And are you saying when people are doing things right the coaches still get it wrong?"

"Ha," laughed the old coach, "I like the way you put that, and yes. When the good things happen, most people are too quick to try to grab up all the credit. Instead, they should be dishing it out. Those are great opportunities to throw out some high fives and 'I am proud of you's,' but instead, most people choose to point the finger back at themselves. As you've already learned, this movement skill isn't easy. But if you get it right, I promise you won't just be a better coach, you'll become the most popular and liked person you know."

"I know I've been guilty of taking the credit, too," said Brian. "There have been a bunch of times when I jumped in to accept credit with both the team and the staff for things that weren't entirely up to me. Thinking back, I now see why some people might have resented me for it and the problems it caused, too. This is one I'm going to have to work on."

"Life is one big practice, kid," said the old man. "The key is to keep showing up and improving. Coachability and availability … remember?"

"Yep, I hear you," said Brian. "But to be clear, the most important movement skill is to know which direction to point my finger when there's a situation involving either credit or blame. And you're saying when things are going good, it's because of their actions, and when things are going bad, it's my fault?"

"Couldn't have said it better myself, kid. Just don't forget the hard part isn't knowing it, it's doing it. And again, this isn't just on the field. This goes for your home, too."

"I was afraid you might say that," laughed Brian. "I am outnumbered three girls to one guy in that house, you know."

The old coach laughed. "Then I have a feeling you're going to get a lot of practice on that movement skill there. Remember, whether it's in your house or on the field, if you accept and live by the idea that players win games and coaches lose them, you will have a much smoother life."

"Trust me," said Brian, "I'm already thinking of a number of situations I could have used that exercise to make my life way smoother. I'll do my best to put it to use right away."

"As long as you remember to look for ways to get recognition for someone else, you're on the right track. And speaking of exercises and work," said the old coach, "now let me show you a few things I know about real training…"

The old coach then led Brian through a great workout. He taught each exercise with detail and patience and seemed to know exactly when to give Brian rest and how to challenge him at the same time. It had been a long time since Brian had let himself just be a student again, and he discovered that he did enjoy learning new things. The workout was also an escape where he had the chance just to focus on his movement and breathing instead of the other things causing stress or worry in his life. As they bowed under the chain on the way out, Brian felt a little more respect for the field and what lessons it taught him. Part of the bow was in honor of the old coach, too.

14

The Secret Move

After the workout with the old coach, Brian headed in to the football offices for an impromptu meeting with Coach Olsen. Brian let the coach know that he had been making progress with his players and was looking forward to some improved play for the big game on Saturday. The coach had commented that he noticed a difference in both the attitude and the play of the linebackers and to keep doing what he was doing. He also mentioned that a few of the other coaches had noticed a change, too. In particular, the offensive line coach had mentioned they had met to go over some ideas on film together. Coach Olsen commended Brian for opening up to work with the other coaches.

For practice that afternoon, the team would be working on some defenses designed to stop the high-powered offense of their rivals lead by their drop-back Heisman-hopeful quarterback, Billy Mitchell. Not only had Mitchell lived up to his Heisman hype with a four-touchdown game the previous week, but there was also talk in the local papers that he would shred Brian's defense this Saturday. This was the extra incentive Coach Olsen hoped would spur his team on to a possible underdog upset.

Before practice, Brian met Marcus in the locker room and the two of them headed out to the practice field early.

"So, when do I get to see the secret you were going to show me?" asked Marcus.

"I see you didn't forget about it, did you?" replied Brian.

"Hard to forget when you leave me hanging like that," Marcus said with a smile.

"Ha, I apologize for that," said Brian. "And while I'm on the topic of apologies, I want to add to the one I gave you yesterday. I know I told you I was sorry for how you were feeling, but I also want you to know that it is my fault."

Brian looked Marcus directly in the eyes when he said this and Marcus just looked down and nodded, kicking at the turf.

"Nah," said Marcus, "you don't have to say that. I just haven't been improving like everyone hoped I would."

"No, Marcus," said Brian. "It's my fault that you haven't been making that improvement. I haven't given you all the tools you need to be your best. And today we're going to start fresh with one of the tools that I think can make a big difference."

"Is this the secret tool?" asked Marcus.

"Think of it more like a secret weapon," said Brian. "I've been thinking a lot the last couple of days about your abilities and style of play. When I was a player, I had a coach who was pretty progressive. Always looking for an edge, he brought in a high-level wrestler to work on some hand fighting drills with our team. I picked it up pretty quick, and I would always stay after and pick his brain about ways I could incorporate fighting into football. As he learned more about my sport, he showed me a number of techniques. A few of them are ones I've used with you and the team before, but there was one in particular that helped me make a few big plays. I can't believe I forgot about it until now. With your arm length and speed, I think it will be perfect for you."

"Sounds great," said Marcus. "So what is it? Is it a swim move? Or some kind of punch technique?"

"Neither," said Brian. "But before I show you this move, I want to tell you a story that the wrestler told me that went along with it. Would you like to hear it?"

"Sure," replied Marcus. "I'm up for anything that will help."

"There was once this 16-year-old boy in Brazil," began Brian, "and he was a regular kid … went to school, played some sports, and liked to have fun. One of his favorite things was to ride his motor scooter around town. Unfortunately, one day while riding he was in a terrible accident. When he awoke in the hospital, he found that due to the severe damage, the doctors were unable to save his left arm and it had to be amputated."

Brian could tell that Marcus was paying his full attention to the story.

"So, imagine," continued Brian, "that just a few years ago, like that boy, you wake up in a hospital missing an arm. Well, just like you might imagine, the boy is devastated. No longer able to do so many of the things he enjoyed and completely self-conscious about his new appearance, the boy withdrew from friends and family and fell into depression. He was eating less and rarely going outside of the house. With his grades plummeting, his single mother was worried. She knew she had to find something for him to become interested in again. Because she knew he once enjoyed sports, she tried to find a sport in which he could still participate. Because of its minimal use of the hands and arms, she settled on soccer and signed him up for a team." Brian paused for a moment, then continued.

"Since soccer was such a popular sport in Brazil, it was her hope it would give him something to live for because she was terrified she was going to lose him. When he tried soccer, although he could move around with the ball, the decreased coordination of trying to sprint with only one arm bothered him, and again, being so self-conscious, he felt like quitting almost as soon as he started. But one day, on the way back from another failed training session, his mother noticed something. At a stop light, she looked over at her son, but something had his attention. When she glanced to see what it was, she noticed he was looking inside the glass windows of a martial arts dojo. She made a mental note to investigate the possibilities of martial arts the next day."

Marcus was still completely engaged, although he had no idea where this story was going.

"I don't know if you know it," Brian continued, "but aside from Japan, the largest population of Japanese people in the world is in Brazil."

"Nope, I had no idea," said Marcus.

"Well, it's true," replied Brian. "And the martial arts studio that the mother visited the next day was a judo dojo run by an old Japanese master. When the mother went inside and met with the master, she told him about her son's accident and current problems. With tears in her eyes she asked, 'Do you think judo could be something for my son?' To that the master replied, 'Miss, I think your son is perfect for judo. If you bring him tomorrow to meet me and he wants to start, I will personally be his sensei.' The mother was excited, but also a little skeptical. 'How much is this going to cost?' she asked the master. 'Nothing,' answered the master. 'I am so sure judo will be able to help your son that I am prepared to train him for free.' The next day, the boy met the master and since he wanted to feel tougher, he agreed to give judo a try. His new sensei said they would train four days per week and he would even have a special judo *gi* made for him that had the left sleeve removed."

Brian could see the story was affecting Marcus as he rubbed his left shoulder with his right hand. Brian kept telling the story with animation and the inflection he had learned from the old coach.

"The sensei and the boy began the training," said Brian. "And at every practice, four days a week, they worked on nothing but methods of defense and only one offensive move. Day in and day out, the boy would spend half the practice learning to stop any attack and then the second half would be spent on a hundred repetitions of just one judo throw. The boy liked the activity and the training started to build his confidence. Month after month, he continued his training of defense and the one move. After over six months of this, one day he went early to practice and knocked on the sensei's office door at the dojo. 'Sensei?' the boy asked.

"'Yes?' answered the sensei.

"'I wanted to talk to you about something,' the boy said. 'I have been coming for a while now and I want to thank you for all the training.'

"'It has been my pleasure to teach you judo,' said the sensei.

"'Well, that's just it,' replied the boy. 'I've been reading books on judo and watched some of the other students, and it seems there are a lot more moves out there that you aren't teaching me. Am I ever going to get to do any of the other fancy moves?' The sensei, staying calm, just raised his hand and said, 'Judo isn't about fancy things. You have to trust in me and my plan for you. Now get back to your training.'

"The boy did as his sensei instructed and spent another six months working on nothing but his defense and that one move. He was becoming so familiar with the move, when he would drift off to sleep, sometimes he would almost throw himself out of his bed performing it! But even with all the hard training, the boy was starting to get bored and went back to the sensei again to question him. 'Sensei,' said the boy, 'now I've been training for well over a year and still I only know one move. Am I ever going to learn any of the others?' And again the answer from the sensei was the same: Trust in him and the process. And again the boy obliged and went back to his hard training.

"After over another six months, the boy couldn't take it any longer. He was tired of the same old routine and had had enough. He went to the sensei again, but this time had something different to tell him. 'Sensei,' said the boy. 'It has now been almost two years of straight training. I have done everything you've asked. But I'm really bored with the same routine. I hate to say this, but I'm thinking about quitting. Unless you can teach me something new, I will probably give up.'"

"Man," said Marcus, "I would've probably given up way before that!"

"Well," said Brian, "wait until you hear this! The boy was worried the sensei would be angered by this decision, but instead a smile crossed his lips. The sensei said, 'I thought you might be feeling this way. And that is why I have a deal for you. I have entered you in the national championships, and if you compete and don't do well, I will allow you to quit. The tournament is in four months and all I ask is that for all the training I have given you, you finish those four months and compete.' The boy was in shock. 'National tournament?' he exclaimed. 'But I've never competed!' The sensei again asked him to trust the process and if they had a deal. Because he had helped the boy from a dark place in his life, he relented and decided there was nothing to lose and went back to his training."

"I don't know if I would do that," said Marcus.

"Me neither," replied Brian, "but keep listening because it gets even better. The boy did his daily training with the sensei and the day of the tournament arrived. There was, of course, a buzz about the one-armed boy who would be competing. No one knew who he was, but he was easily recognizable in his custom one-armed *gi*. Then it was time for his first match. The boy was both nervous and scared. Right before stepping onto the mats, he turned to his sensei and said, 'I don't know what to do.' The sensei, ever relaxed, said, 'You only know one move. I would suggest you do that!'"

"Ha," laughed Marcus. "Good advice."

Brian continued the story, becoming even more animated. "The match began and to the boy's surprise, he realized that no matter what the other judoka tried to do for an attack, the boy had a counter for it. All that defensive work had made him almost impossible to throw. Seeing a little opening, the boy went for his move and BOOM! He landed a full throw and won the match!"

Marcus smiled widely as Brian continued.

"The crowd was a little stunned, but now everyone was watching him. As the tournament continued, the boy started to rack up more victories and more confidence. Match after match deeper into the tournament the boy would keep relying on his defense to set up his one move. And every time he would go for it, it seemed the other fighters had no answer. After each victory, he became the crowd favorite until the whole audience was on its feet to see what he was going to do next. The boy was tired, but he was giving it his all. He won again and not only found himself going to the final, but also optimistic about his chances.

"That was, until he encountered the person he would be fighting in the final. Before the match, the other fighter attempted to psych the boy out by saying, 'Hey, I'm not going to take it easy on you like all the other people you fought today. Be ready for the final, because I am going to tear off your other arm!' The angry judoka thought he had succeeded in intimidating the boy. The boy, unfortunately, thought so, too."

"What a jerk!" said Marcus, getting closer to Brian so as not to miss a word of the story. "So did he win it?"

"Well," continued Brian, "the match began and the angry judoka was really roughing the boy up. You know, giving him cheap shots to the face and body and just really playing rough. But no matter how he tried to attack, the boy stayed calm and had a defensive answer for his offense. The boy kept mounting a successful defense, but because the judoka was tiring him out, he was running out of time and losing by an advantage. He knew he had to do something or he would lose. With only seconds left, the boy fully committed and went for it. He got halfway into position for the move, but the angry judoka was ready for it. Then in what seemed like an eternity, both fighters were locked in a stalemate, equally balancing each other so neither one could move."

As he was telling the story, Brian put his hands on Marcus in the same way he was describing and started to show him the next part of the move.

"Pulling with all he had and relying on the technique the sensei had taught him, the boy started hopping on one foot, slowly getting himself closer to and twisting the body of his opponent. With each hop, the roar of the crowd rose. And then just before time elapsed, the boy off-balanced the judoka enough and threw him for a half-point and the victory!"

At that moment, Brian performed the move on Marcus by off-balancing him, gently directing him to the ground.

"The crowd went insane!" Brian yelled with his hands up. "They rushed the mats, held the boy in the air, and paraded him around the arena. Tears of joy were streaming down the boy's face. He was interviewed, tons of photos were taken, and then he collected his gold medal to the delight of the crowd."

"That is some story," said Marcus with a smile.

"You didn't even get the best part yet," said Brian. "In the locker room after the hoopla had died down, the sensei and the boy were alone together. It was then that the boy noticed the 'I told you so' smile on the sensei's face. Suspicious of what had transpired that day, the boy asked his teacher, 'Sensei, was that real out there today? Or was it a setup? Do you think those other guys went easy on me?' With that question, the smile instantly disappeared from the sensei's face and was replaced with a stern and serious look. 'Judo,' said the sensei, 'is an art of honor. No one let you win today.'

"'But how could I have won?' asked the boy, 'when I only know one move?'

"'Son,' he said, 'you have mastered one of the most difficult throws in all of judo.'

"'Yes,' said the boy, 'but I still only know that one move.'

"'Well,' replied the sensei with a sinister grin, 'about that one move ... '

"'Yes, sensei?' said the boy.

"'There is something I never told you about it.'

"'Yes, sensei?' repeated the boy, very interested.

"The sensei continued, 'Did you know the only way to defend that one move ... '

"'Yes, sensei?' said the boy, leaning ever closer to his teacher.

"'Did you know the only way that someone can counter that one move ... ' said the sensei, and again the boy replied more eagerly with his inquiry, 'Yes, sensei?'

"But the sensei continued as if he didn't hear him, getting louder, 'Did you know the only way someone can protect himself from that one move ... '

"'Yes, sensei?' said the boy, getting louder, too.

"Finally, the sensei ended his explanation with, 'Did you know the only way to ever stop that move ... *is someone would have to grab on to your left arm!*'"

When Marcus got the lesson, he started jumping up and down with excitement and clapping. "Wow! That is one of the best stories I've ever heard. Is all that stuff that happened really true?"

Brian replied, "I don't know if it's true, Marcus, but there are stories that happen like that every day. There are always people out there who turn their greatest weakness into their greatest strength. And that's why I remembered the story for today. Because I'm going to teach you one move that will possibly help you do it, too."

"Enough already," exclaimed Marcus. "I am ready for this!"

"Okay," said Brian, "I was watching film of you and wondering why you were getting beat by some of the offensive linemen on blocking. I know you are super strong for your size and have the speed, and I couldn't figure out why you were getting shut down once these guys got a hold of you."

"Ha," said Marcus, "I know what you're talking about. It gets me angry because holding is a penalty, isn't it?"

"In theory," answered Brian, "but you know they're going to hold when they lock up with you. I was sharing that with the offensive line coach for ideas and that's when he showed me something on film about you."

"What?" asked Marcus.

"Your arms," replied Brian. "They're too short."

"What?" said Marcus. "My arms look normal to me."

"That's not what I mean," said Brian. "Your arms are long, but not as long as a 6'6″ offensive lineman's. And as a result, when they go for their punch on you to lock you up, they're able to get their hands on you from a greater distance before you can swat them off since their arms are longer. So, if you're unable to keep their hands off you, they are able to nullify you with a hold."

"I see what you mean." said Marcus. "And it's been frustrating to feel powerless when I get the chance to rush or blitz. Man, I would really love a few sacks this season."

"That's where the secret move comes in!" said Brian excitedly. "When the other coach got me to realize the issue with your arms, I went back to some of my old notes from the hand fighting drills I had learned. And that's when I found the 'steering wheel.' Yes, your arms may be shorter than a lineman's, but they are *perfect* for this!"

"I'm not gonna hit a guy with a steering wheel, am I?" joked Marcus.

"No," said Brian, "but I'm going to teach you how to turn an offensive lineman into one!"

Brian then explained the steering wheel technique to Marcus. This was a move that could be used only when an offensive lineman had locked up with a player. By using both hands against just one of the lineman's arms and driving that arm upward and sideways, Brian explained how a linebacker could off-balance and overpower a bigger and heavier lineman to steer him where he wanted. If done correctly, this move could create havoc in the backfield for a quarterback and disrupt a play. Although Marcus was initially skeptical, when Brian performed the move on him, Marcus could immediately feel the value of the technique. Once he had Marcus's trust, Brian then explained and demonstrated the finer points of the execution of the technique from grip to direction of force. Then Brian had Marcus practice the move on him over and over until he started to get the hang of it.

"Man," said Marcus, "I can't wait to use this move!"

"Not so fast, Marcus," said Brian. "Don't forget about the judo story. The boy didn't just learn the move in a day and win the tournament. He practiced thousands of repetitions over a long period of time to become great. This practice allowed him to learn the strategy and timing behind the move, too. Even though some players just try to get faster and stronger to improve in football, you cannot forget about the importance of the skills of your position. You said you wanted to be great at something. I am challenging you to be a black belt linebacker. And if you accept, I promise I will do whatever I can to help you get there."

"Yes, sensei!" said Marcus with a bow.

"Ha!" laughed Brian. "Enough of that, and let's get in as many reps as we can before practice starts. There's no lamb for the lazy wolf."

Brian and Marcus practiced the move over and over until the other players started making their way out onto the field. As they came out to watch, Brian told them, to Marcus's surprise, that Marcus would be doing some extra work with them on technique. Then Brian stepped out and Marcus started showing some of his teammates the move.

"And after practice," said Marcus to them, "have I got a story to tell you guys … "

15

The Holy Grail

Brian's linebacking core had another great practice that was filled with high fives and enthusiasm. The positive energy was spilling over to the other players on the team as well, and the coaching staff was getting more optimistic about the big game on Saturday. Although they were considered a 20-point underdog, Brian could tell they were not the same team as the week before.

After practice, the linebackers, led by Marcus, stayed to do some extra work on hand fighting. Brian saw there were some new and important connections forming and excused himself from the group so he could still get to the Trackside Diner on time.

Again Brian made it a few minutes early hoping to beat the old coach to their usual table. And once again, the old coach was already there waiting with a smile on his face.

"Another good day?" asked the old coach.

"You said it, Coach!" replied Brian as he pulled out his golden notebook and placed it on the table. "The team has really been on fire. They are working together, the high fives are happening naturally, and I'm especially proud of Marcus for opening up and becoming a leader with the linebackers."

"Did you tell Marcus you're proud of him?" asked the old coach.

"I told him during the paper exercise," said Brian, "but I haven't told him since. Ugh. I see what you mean now, Coach. Sometimes we see something we like, are proud of it, but only say it in our heads as if the person should just know it. Thanks for the reminder. I'll keep working on saying it when I feel it."

"Don't worry," said the old coach, "That's what I meant when we talked about making mistakes. Nothing is ever a failure until you give up working at it. Just keep the Golden Rule in mind and those five powerful words will start to happen as naturally as the high fives."

Brian pulled off the black band and flipped open his golden notebook to show the old coach some of the ideas he had been writing down. He told the old coach about the judo story and the move that he shared with Marcus.

"I copied your idea of telling a story," said Brian. "Your stories have been really helpful for me to learn a point and that's when I remembered the judo story. I think it really hit home with Marcus, and since he shared the story with the other players, they're all thinking about how to make some of their weaknesses into strengths."

"You didn't copy me," said the old coach. "Humans have been telling stories since the beginning of our existence. I believe we're hardwired as humans to remember stories and pass them down. But regardless what the science says, I know there are few people who can resist a good story. So, I've always made it a point to collect my favorites and then share them when the time is right."

"I think this notebook may become a place where I'll be keeping my best ones, Coach," said Brian.

"Great idea," said the old coach. "I used to have one that looked just like it. Now, speaking of ideas, I want to share another important coaching skill with you that few people understand. Today you showed Marcus a secret weapon for football. Tonight I want to give you another secret weapon for coaching."

"I'm all ears," said Brian.

"You gotta be more than that for this skill, kid," said the old coach. "This skill doesn't just involve the six inches between your ears, this one involves your heart, too. Without both your heart and mind in your coaching, you will never be able to properly carry out the Golden Rule."

"So, are you saying you have to care about your athletes?" asked Brian.

"Of course you have to care for your athletes," said the old coach, "but I'm talking about an idea bigger and deeper than that. It goes without saying that every coach should care about the people under his watch. But that caring could be selfish just to make sure to get a win or for the coach to make himself look good. Any coach can be selfish. I'm talking about the skill that allows you to use the Golden Rule to become selfless. You're already doing it; I just want to make you aware of it so you can get even better."

"So then let me have it," said Brian.

"Ha!" said the old coach. "You already have it, kid. Everybody does. You just have to improve it. We've already talked about the Golden Rule and how a great coach gets more excited or enthusiastic about someone else than himself. But as you've already learned, this isn't easy to do. You have to actually wake up a part of your brain that will help your heart to do what it was designed to do. In order to be more enthusiastic about someone else than yourself, you have to be able to put yourself in their shoes. So, the skill I am talking about is *empathy*."

"Empathy?" said Brian as he wrote the word down in his notebook. "To be honest, Coach, I've heard the word, but I don't really understand what it means."

"Not many people do, Brian," said the old coach. "And that's why so many people are lousy at it and the Golden Rule. To show you what I mean, I'm going to use your experience with Marcus this week. When you did the enthusIASM paper exercise, how did it make you feel?"

"Like I told you," said Brian, "when he told me about his dad and the place he was from and the pressure he was under, I really felt bad for him."

"Exactly!" said the old coach. "You see, that's called *sympathy*. You show sympathy when you feel bad *for* someone. So when you tell someone who has had a tragedy that you 'feel sorry for them for their loss,' you are exhibiting sympathy. Sympathy isn't the same as empathy."

"So how then have I shown empathy with Marcus this week?"

"You did it today!" answered the old coach. "And that's why you went the extra mile and told him the story and showed him the move. You see, you didn't lose your father when you were young or grow up in a depressed neighborhood. But you were a linebacker who felt the pressure when you didn't perform well. When it comes to Marcus's challenges on the field, you were able to put yourself in his shoes. As a result, you did extra work and enacted the Golden Rule. Sympathy was when you felt bad *for* him. You showed empathy when you started to feel bad *with* him."

"So, is sympathy a bad thing?" asked Brian.

"No," answered the old coach, "that isn't what I'm saying at all. A person should, of course, have both. And unfortunately, many people aren't good at either one of them. But as a coach, empathy is going to push you to be the best. It's also going to make coaching both more pleasurable and painful."

"Painful?" repeated Brian.

"Well, maybe I should have said *richer*," said the old coach. "What I mean is that when you become more empathetic, you are going to feel the failures of your people with much more emotion. So, it's easier not to turn up your empathy. That protective mechanism is why people probably don't use it. But remember, the successes are much more emotional, too. Overall, when you become a more empathetic coach, your experiences, good or bad, are richer. When you develop the skill of empathy, coaching doesn't become something you do *to* someone, it becomes something you do *with* them."

"I get it," said Brian. "And that's exactly how I felt with Marcus today. When he was practicing, I wasn't just telling him what to do. I could actually feel him going through the movements, too. But is empathy something you can really improve? I wasn't exactly raised in a house full of empathy. Maybe it's a nature versus nurture thing?"

"Wow," said the old coach, "I didn't think we would be having this discussion. But since you asked, I do believe that for most attributes, genes and environment play a role in the expression of things like empathy. But regardless if you were born the most empathetic person, I believe it's something you can improve. And I know once again because I did it.

"There was a time when I was only concerned with myself and where I was going. As a result, my coaching style was more of a dictator than an ally. It wasn't until a colleague of mine showed me an article that explained how scientists had found there are centers of your brain that light up when you become more empathetic. And when those centers are activated more often, they actually got bigger! When I heard that, I stopped believing I was born to be a tough guy and thought of my brain more like a muscle. So if I could do exercises to make my biceps bigger, I thought I could exercise my empathy to make those sections of my brain bigger, too."

"I did notice you have a pretty big head," joked Brian. "But seriously, what things did you do to improve your empathy?"

"Well," continued the old coach, "I learned that empathy isn't just taught, it's also caught. So in addition to taking the time to imagine the situation that my athletes were going through to attempt to understand them better, I did two other things that helped me to improve the skill. First, I had a friend tell me that every time I was working with an athlete, I should imagine some words on his or her forehead and never forget those words while I was coaching them."

"Did you just pick any words?" asked Brian.

"At first I did," said the old coach, "but eventually I settled on two simple words that never failed me no matter who I was working with. Those two words were *help me*. In essence, those words became the greatest reminder of my job description as a coach that I was always supposed to help take someone where they wanted to go that they couldn't get there themselves."

Inspired, Brian wrote the words *help me* in his golden notebook.

"The second thing that I used to improve my empathy was I surrounded myself with people who seemed to exhibit the skill more naturally than I did. I would watch how they would interact with people, ask them about it, and then emulate them. Over time, as my use of empathy got better, so did my results and my relationships."

"I have a couple people in mind who I can question about that," said Brian.

"Who are they?" asked the old coach.

"Well, you might not believe this, but it's my wife and mother-in-law!" laughed Brian.

"I'm not surprised at all," replied the old coach. "In my experience, women tend to show more empathy than men. And with two daughters at home, I suggest you get working on it, kid."

"As usual, you're right, Coach." said Brian, realizing that many of the arguments and challenges with his wife and kids could be traced back to his lack of empathy to understand the situation. "And I think my wife will get a kick out of me recruiting her mom for some empathy lessons. Well, that's after she gets over the initial shock and asks me what I've done with her real husband."

"That's funny," said the old coach. "But I think communicating about those things with her is only going to make things better. Just like it did with Marcus."

"I have a feeling you're right again, Coach."

"Good," said the old coach. "Because feeling is what empathy is all about. And I believe that only once you have really mastered the skill of empathy will you ever be able to find the 'Holy Grail' of coaching."

"Do you have a King Arthur story for me now?" asked Brian.

"No," said the old coach with a smile, "but if you have some Holy Grail experiences like I have in my career, you will surely feel like a king."

"So what is it?" asked Brian as he leaned in for the answer.

"Once I'd really done the deep work on coaching," said the old coach, "the grail became my obsession. Once I understood my job description, internalized the Golden Rule, and was building my empathy, I really focused on my athletes and their results. It was time to dedicate myself solely to them. And to test whether my skills really had an influence on those results, I started to analyze my interactions with those athletes. I became a believer in the power of a coach to influence. But I saw it didn't happen all the time, so I strove to crack the code of producing consistent high-level results. Those perfect moments were so tough to find, that's why I called it the Holy Grail."

"So what is it?" asked Brian impatiently.

"The Holy Grail of coaching is to do and say the right thing, in the right way, at the right time, to the right person, that produces the right result," said the old coach. "In the millions of interactions I've had with athletes over the years, there were times when it happened and others when it didn't. Like I taught you, I learned to point the finger of blame at myself when the result my athlete wanted didn't occur. When I showed empathy, it helped me get them even closer to their goal."

"I know exactly what you mean," said Brian looking down as he was writing down the old coach's definition of the Holy Grail in his notebook:

do and say the right thing,
in the right way,
at the right time,
to the right person,
to get the right result.

Then he looked back at the old coach and said, "There have been a few times when I said just the right thing that was what one of my athletes needed to hear at that moment, and they shocked me and themselves with a performance or play that was completely unexpected."

"That's the grail I'm talking about! And how did it feel when it happened?"

"Not many feelings like it," answered Brian. "It was a combo of pride and happiness and achievement, for sure. Come to think of it, I would love more of those."

"Then for the next few days," said the old coach, "it's your turn to put everything I've taught you to work. And I mean both on the field and at home. I keep telling you the only way to get good at this stuff is to do it. Amateurs do things enough times just to get them right. Professionals do things so many times they can't get them wrong."

"I'm ready to put this stuff to the test," said Brian, patting his notebook on the table. "So workout at the same time tomorrow?"

To Brian's surprise, the old coach shook his head. "My work is almost done here. Just like any coach, you have to eventually trust in your athlete and let them take the field and play. I have taught you the most important things I know about coaching. Now it's time for you to use them."

Brian was really upset by this but tried not to show it. He understood the old coach had been spending a lot of time and energy on him. And he also realized that their interactions were still mainly all take for Brian and no give. Even though Brian had only known the old coach for a few days, it seemed like he'd known him for much longer. Maybe it was the coach's skill of empathy that allowed him to completely understand Brian. Whatever it was, Brian knew he had become a better coach and person after spending such a short time with the coach and he didn't want it to end.

"I'm sorry to hear that, Coach," said Brian. "I was really enjoying our time together. It's been a while since I had somebody to talk to. It's been a while since I felt like I had a friend."

"I've really enjoyed our time, too," replied the old coach. "More than you can imagine. But I knew going into this, I only had a short time to work. But I want to thank you for reminding me of my purpose and giving this old coach a reason to get up early again. You've really surprised me how fast you've learned and put the stuff I've shared to use. Now it's your turn to use my lessons with someone else. Take what you have learned and put it to use. I would suggest you keep taking notes in your notebook and see what else you can figure out on your own about coaching."

"I will," said Brian.

"And as for having friends, kid … you have a team of athletes and coaches and a family at home who are dying to be those people for you. I suggest you let them."

Brian extended his arm and shook the hand of the old coach. "Thank you," said Brian sincerely.

"My pleasure," responded the old coach. And the handshake lasted longer than usual because neither man wanted to let go first.

Brian must have been visibly upset when he walked in the door at home because Kelly immediately picked up on his mood.

"Tough day at work?" asked Kelly as she gave him a kiss hello.

"Work is going great," replied Brian. "You know that coach I've been telling you about? I just have a feeling I won't see him again. The stuff he's been sharing has been so helpful; I wish we had more time."

"I'm sorry to hear that," said Kelly. "For the way you have been acting lately, I wish I could get a chance to thank him in person."

"I think he would get a kick out of that," said Brian.

Just then, Jenny and Jaime came running in to say hello. After their hugs, each one of them sat on each of Brian's feet and wrapped their arms and legs around his lower leg. They giggled wildly as Brian walked around the house with them hanging on. Their screams got even louder as Brian marched over with them to Kelly and gave her a second hello kiss.

Before dinner, Brian and the girls went into the backyard to kick the soccer ball around. Since Jenny had started playing soccer that year, Brian was excited to practice with her. When they got outside, however, Jenny was the one who didn't seem so excited.

"Hey, Jenny-girl," inquired Brian, "don't you feel like playing soccer today?"

"Not really," said Jenny sheepishly. "I'm not sure if I want to play soccer anymore."

"What?" replied Brian. "But I thought you were having lots of fun playing."

"That's just it, Daddy," answered Jenny. "The coach doesn't make practice fun anymore. There's just a lot of yelling. And I don't feel like he likes me."

Brian immediately recognized Jenny's coach needed to hear the Golden Rule, too. He figured there were probably tens of thousands of coaches out there who could benefit from the lessons of the old coach.

"Don't worry, Jenny," said Brian. "Sometimes coaches make mistakes. Sports should always be fun, but sometimes coaches get too serious. Don't worry, I'll make sure to talk to your coach about it."

Brian and Jenny kicked the ball around and worked on some skills. Brian took Jenny's complaint to heart and made sure to keep the time they had together fun. He also let her know he was proud of her for being so honest.

After dinner and the bedtime rituals with the girls, Brian and Kelly were in bed getting ready to go to sleep. Kelly was doing some last-minute designs on her computer and Brian was skimming through his golden notebook. Inspired by the lessons inside the notebook, Brian decided to ask Kelly about work.

"How's that new design project going?" asked Brian.

"It's going okay, Kelly replied, surprised by his question. "Do you really want to know about it?"

"Yes," Brian said. "Even though I may not often say it, I'm really impressed with a lot of the event designs you put together."

"Oh, really?" said Kelly. "Which one impressed you?"

"You don't believe me?" asked Brian with a laugh. "I really liked those promotional banners and matching brochures you made for that mortgage banking company's event. And to show I do pay attention, I also liked the custom backpacks for that fitness event and the cool keychains for the university."

"Wow, now I'm impressed!" smiled Kelly.

"Sorry for not always acting interested in what you do, Kell," said Brian. "I want you to know what you do is just as important as football. And I am proud to have a wife as talented as you."

Because she hadn't heard things like this in a long time from Brian, Kelly was silent for a few moments. "Are you sure you aren't sick or something?" she asked finally, with a suspicious grin.

"Never better, babe," replied Brian. "Never better."

"Sorry if I'm not used to this," said Kelly.

"It's not your fault," answered Brian, "It's mine. It's not just about the kids. I need to do a better job showing I'm enthusiastic about what you're doing, too. And I'm going to keep working at letting you know it."

"What have you done with my husband?" Kelly joked as she rolled over and gave him a hug.

Brian laughed. "If you don't recognize me now, wait until I tell you I also want to spend some quality time with your mother!"

16

Do the Work

On Thursday and Friday, the energy on campus began to change. More people were wearing the colors of the university around campus and trailers filled with both alumni and television stations had begun to already appear in the 80,000-seat stadium's parking lot. So it is with the big rivalry games of college football.

During the last two days before the game, Brian was committed to putting all the coaching lessons he had learned from the old coach to work. He also kept his golden notebook in his front pocket and reviewed what he had written over the past few days as a reminder to take action on some of the new skills. He also took the old coach's advice and wrote down his own ideas on coaching when he experienced them. Writing down his ideas really did help Brian to internalize them. It was as if there was a connection from his hand to his brain that was helping him to etch these coaching lessons in his mind.

On Thursday before practice, Brian and Marcus took the other linebackers through the enthusIASM paper exercise. There was so much talk about it, the other players on the team wanted in on it, too. Brian was impressed by Marcus taking a leadership role on the exercise and let him know about it immediately with the five most powerful words.

Brian saw an even increased power with the clarity that the exercise created. Not only did each player become clearer about why they were playing college football, but by sharing their stories with the rest of the team, there was also an increased layer of team trust that hadn't existed before. And with that trust there was a different level of caring. Brian realized the old coach had been right again – all it took to bring about this caring was a little extra time.

Once Brian and the other coaches knew where the players wanted to go, it was their turn to show some enthusiasm to help them get there. Brian saw the new enthusiasm showed by the defense was now spilling over to the offense as well. Once the entire team started taking the Golden Rule to heart – *you have to be more enthusiastic about someone else than yourself* – the real magic started to happen. When they were a team of individuals, practice had often been filled with trash talk and taunts to antagonize one another. Now drills were complemented with cheers and high fives for a job well done.

But on one particular moment during Thursday's practice, Brian had to take another profound note about a lesson he learned. When the defense was replicating the defense for the upcoming game with the offense, Marcus put a hard tackle on the star receiver of the team. This time after the tackle, instead of jumping around and pointing to himself to garner attention for a nice play, Marcus's first move was to help the receiver off the ground. Brian pulled out his notebook and wrote this down:

> *The best way for a coach to become stronger is to lift someone else up.*

But practice wasn't the only place that Brian found the coaching combination was working. In just a week, he could see that his relationship with Kelly and the girls was improving, too. Athletes aren't the only people who have two tanks. Brian discovered that everyone has them and made a point to spend some time filling the emotional tank for the girls, too. Brian stayed present at dinner with Kelly and paid attention when she explained how her day was and what she was feeling. Just by sitting back, keeping eye contact and making sure not to interrupt, he felt closer to Kelly than he had in years and was reminded why he fell in love with her in the first place. With the girls, he put both the phone and playbooks down for some reading and games with them. And that night, he made sure to single out one thing he was proud of them for and let them know it right before they went to bed. Brian saw firsthand that putting your kids to bed with a smile on their face feeling good about themselves was one of the nicest things a parent can do.

Although he was working on being more coachable and had made himself way more available, Brian was still making mistakes. But those mistakes were no longer frustrating him; they were now fascinating him. For example, when Brian yelled at one of the players and saw that it had a negative effect on the athlete's performance and demeanor, he asked him after practice what he believed would be the best way to coach him. That athlete let him know he didn't respond well to yelling and immediately their understanding led to a stronger connection.

No matter what, Brian found himself constantly searching for opportunities to give out some positive feedback or credit for a job well done. His high five was getting better and becoming a more natural part of him. In fact, when he high-fived the lady behind the counter at the coffee shop, even she responded with a smile. The power of the Golden Rule was taking effect all around him.

Taking the blame for people's mistakes, however, wasn't as easy. Brian found that he was much better at pointing out people's errors and affixing blame than he was at pointing back at himself how he could fix the problem. But, just like that hall-of-fame hitter in baseball, Brian remembered you have to strike out sometimes even when you are thinking about hitting home runs.

Friday was an especially light day before the game, and Brian used the time to focus a little individual time on Kelly. Since they'd had kids, he realized that they never really had any alone time anymore. Although Kelly often mentioned it, Brian hadn't been able to put himself in her shoes. But now he finally understood. And he wanted to make sure she knew that football was not more important than her or their family. Although the day before a game can usually be high stress and busy, Brian took Kelly to lunch for what he called a "date" before he had to meet up with the team that evening. At lunch they talked about what she wanted to do with her career. And again Brian did a good job at listening to her answers. He realized this action had a positive effect on both of them because not only was Kelly smiling as she excitedly shared her dreams, but watching her explain her enthusiasm for the future made him smile, too. Later, after Brian returned to his office, he wrote down in his notebook:

> *Empathy is first about spending time thinking about where someone is coming from. Only then can you help them get to where they want to go. And the only way to "hear" where someone wants to go is to take the time to listen.*

That night, as was customary for a big home game, Brian and the team assembled and checked in to a local hotel near campus. This gave Brian a final chance to reflect on what he had learned. Though the two days raced by like a whirlwind, Brian did think about the old coach often. He wished they'd had more time together and was grateful for the lessons the old coach had shared so selflessly with him. Brian felt some regret that he never took the time to find out more about the old coach or what he needed. He promised himself to make sure other people came first in his future interactions. But Brian figured out through all his work those last two days that one of the greatest lessons of the old coach was the one that only now he could see. He took the time Friday evening in his hotel room to write the idea down in his notebook:

> *It's not what a coach gets a person to do when they are with them, but what they do when they are not with them that demonstrates the true influence and skill of that coach.*

Before he turned in for the night, Brian sat at the little table, thinking about the outcome of the game. He knew his team had improved, but he also believed the press's evaluation that they were still considered under-dogs. Brian felt the pressure that came with the fear for his job security. He was keenly aware that if his team lost, his job might be on the line. But he was confident that even if they lost the game, it would not be the measure of his value. This newfound confidence came because he knew he had been working on himself to become more valuable as a coach and as a person. To prove this to himself, after he put the playbooks away, Brian pulled out his little notebook and wrote down everything he had learned over the past week. The words seemed to flow from his brain onto the pages:

What Is A Coach?
The coach is a model for the team. His best teaching skill is by example. When modeling correctly, the coach sets the values, standards, and expectations for his athletes.

With these in place, the athlete will understand the behaviors required to be his best.

So, the first person the coach has to get something out of is himself.

As a coach you have to know where you are going before you can lead anyone else there.

To lead someone, you first need your own direction. Your direction comes from the intersection of your passion and purpose.

Passion puts you on your authentic path. Purpose keeps you moving down the road when things get tough. You need to be crystal clear on both. When you have clarity, your days and decisions all become easier. And others will line up confidently to follow.

Once you have people following you down the coach's path, you have to get good at getting lost. Lost in the lives of those people. A coach knows it's not about him. Coaching is about them.

So, for you to be successful as a coach, you have to worry about making other people successful first. And if you want to be the best coach in the world, you must do everything in your power to bring out the best in someone else!

Bringing out the best in others requires a coach to listen.

A coach must listen first if he ever expects anyone to listen to him. Since people are motivated by different things; the coach has to learn these things and individually use them to get high-level performance. A coach must constantly be listening in order to find the key to unlocking someone else's best effort.

Once the coach knows what the person wants, he should employ enthusiasm to help the person get there, knowing a coach's best motive is someone else's best interests.

To take someone where they want to go, the coach must constantly seek to close the gap between where they are and what they want. Closing that gap will help people produce victories on the field. But the greater victories will be the victories over themselves, reducing fear and frustration while increasing confidence and courage.

On this journey, a coach should spend more time focused on the small successes than the tiny mistakes. This involves the right use of feedback. So, the coach is not just there to see potential. The real job is getting the student to reach it. A skill of a great coach is to deliver the right feedback at the right time. If a coach sees something to be proud of, that coach should let the athlete know about it immediately. What gets rewarded will get repeated.

A coach also can't get too caught up in wins and losses. If victories on the field create defeats for the coach at home, that will be the biggest and most costly loss. Although sports can be very serious, the coach should remember to keep training and competing fun, and to never forget that family comes first.

Coaching is not about what you get. It's about what you give back to future generations. A coach is ultimately there to improve not just the skills for the game for a season, but also the skills for the game called life. Coaching is a lifelong pursuit. A coach has to teach with enthusiasm like there is no tomorrow, but remember to learn, train, love, and improve like he is going to live forever.

Proud of what he had written, Brian felt this manifesto would be a guide he would follow for the rest of his coaching career. But as the clock struck 11:30 p.m., he realized his team still had a job to do tomorrow. Yes, there were still the butterflies he usually got the night before a game. In fact, Brian noticed the butterflies flew around more vigorously since he'd become a coach than when he was an athlete. But instead of the usual fear and anxiety he felt the night before a game, Brian fell asleep reflecting on what he'd written down, with a peace of mind that only such clarity on passion and purpose can produce.

17

Game Day

Game day for a college football team is filled with tradition. After all, one would expect there to be a number of traditions when two colleges have played each other for almost 100 years.

Brian and the team woke up and reported for a team breakfast at 8 a.m. Already you could feel the adrenaline starting to flow as the players loaded up on eggs, bacon, and oatmeal. A former star player for the team who was now doing a good bit of motivational speaking gave a speech to the team.

He focused on what it meant to be a player for the college and experiences from his four different times playing against the team's main rivals. The main thesis of his speech reminded the players to "make the most important thing the most important thing." Of course, his finale focused on the fact that this game was the most important game on the schedule.

During the speech at breakfast, Brian was sitting with the coaches, but after it ended he made sure to make his way over to Marcus to see how he was feeling.

"You ready for this?" asked Brian.

"It's always easy to get up for games like this," replied Marcus. "But I'm really hoping we do something special today. The guys have been working hard and I wouldn't want to see it go backward with a loss."

"Nobody wants to lose," said Brian. "But as you're going to find out eventually, Marcus, you can't control whether you win or lose all the time. But you can always control your effort and enthusiasm. I'm just asking you to focus on those and give all you got. So tell me, are you hungry?"

"Nah," said Marcus. "I already ate some, but I'm never able to eat too much before a game."

"Ha!" laughed Brian. "I didn't mean that kind of hunger. I mean, are you hungry to play at your best today? Are you still hungry to be great?"

"Oh," smiled Marcus back, "My bad. Yeah, you know I'm hungry."

"Well," said Brian. "That isn't going to be enough. Every person on that field today is going to be hungry. I want to hear that you are *starving!*"

With an even bigger smile Marcus said, "I am starving. And I've been that way for a while."

"Then," said Brian as he put his hand on Marcus's shoulder with a strong grip, "I want you to go out there today and *eat!*"

Brian made his way around the table and told the other players what he thought they might need to hear. After breakfast was over, the team went back to their rooms to get dressed into suits and ties for the trip over to the stadium.

It was tradition to get dressed up in the finest clothes before the game. One of the original coaches for the team believed that "if you dressed good, you felt good. And if you felt good on game day, you played good." So, after the team cleaned up, and cleaned out their rooms, they were all checked out and the team boarded the charter buses and headed over to the stadium. As the players and coaches looked out the windows, they could already see the streets were lined with fans cheering them on as the buses drove past. Some players were conversing and obviously energized by the action going on around them and others chose to sit in solitude with headphones listening to the music that inspired them most. Marcus was one of those players sitting alone, nervously getting himself ready for the game ahead.

After slowly making their way through the crowded streets, the buses made the turn off the main campus strip, leaving the carnival-like atmosphere and entering a guarded gate that allowed the buses to drive into the bowels of the stadium. The players disembarked and made their way to the locker room.

Each player had a seat in front of his personal locker, and with some music starting to blare in the background, each player began his custom ritual for getting on his gear. Some hit the training room to be taped, while others taped themselves. Once they were into most of their gear minus shoulder pads and jerseys, the chaplain led the team in prayer. Then it was more prep for the game as players, press, trainers, and coaches all moved around the locker room like buzzing bees. As the time approached for the players to take the field for warmups, the team donned everything but their helmets. Their armor was almost complete.

Before they took the field for the first time, Head Coach Olsen delivered a final pep talk, another tradition. Always good for an inspirational story, he had one ready for the big game. As he walked to the center of the team, each huddled around him on a knee over the team's famous logo on the floor, he held up his hand with a thick 5-foot piece of rope for the entire team to see.

"Today is a big day, gentlemen," began Coach Olsen. "No one has to remind you about that. But I want to remind you of something bigger. Something more important."

As he turned in the center of the circle, making eye contact with each player listening in silence, he continued,

"I am not going to lie to you. I didn't know if this team had what it took to be a winner. Sure, we have the talent, but when the season started a few weeks ago, I still thought something was missing."

This sent a shock wave of emotion through the team, but before they could doubt themselves, Coach Olsen continued his speech, his voice growing louder until it was bouncing off the locker room walls. "But these last few weeks, I have seen some changes. I have watched players giving more effort. Not just in hitting each other, but in supporting each other, too. I have watched many of you start to learn how to lift each other up. I have started to see you grab and hold the rope." With that statement, he raised the rope into the air for dramatic effect. And with a locker room full of giant men so silent you could hear a pin drop, it was clear the effect was working.

"What does 'hold the rope' mean?" boomed Coach Olsen from the center of the huddle. "Well, to explain, I want you to imagine you're hanging over the edge of a cliff by a rope. Imagine being hundreds of feet in the air hanging onto that rope, scared to death." Coach Olsen paused to let the imagery take hold in the players' minds.

"Now," continued Coach Olsen, "I want you to imagine the other side of the rope is coming loose. It's going to break, and you have to choose someone to hold onto that rope or you are going to fall. You have to believe in someone enough to hold that rope and save your life! A few weeks ago, I was worried that we didn't have a team that would grab and hold the rope for each other. And I know you know what I'm talking about. But now, look around." Again, Coach Olsen paused to let the players make eye contact with one another.

"I know you have teammates who would hold the rope for you!" he continued. "But you have to believe it. You have to believe in each other! You have to know there are players here who you would grab onto the rope and hold with all you've got! Holding without fear of pain or injury. Gripping that rope until their hands came off!" As he said this you could see the words having effect. Some players were now swaying side to side while others had looks of both anger and emotion.

"You gotta trust that guy in the trenches next to you," went on Coach Olsen. "You gotta love him," and raising the rope once again, "and to love him means you will hold the rope!"

Coach Olsen paused again, then continued. "I believe this team is building that kind of trust. I want you to think right now about the people who have been holding the rope for you. Not just your teammates and friends. But your parents. Your coaches. Today is the day to honor them and give your best." Brian and Marcus made quick eye contact at that point and Marcus gave Brian a nod.

"This is a big game, and in this game someone may need to step up and grab the rope for someone else. You hold onto the rope until the bitter end, men, and it will be enough. Great things happen for teams that are prepared to hold the rope. I have coached a lot of teams over the years, I think this is one of those teams. Now everyone bring it in!"

With Coach Olsen still in the center of the huddle, the emotional players all stood up and reached in with an attempt to touch a piece of the 5-foot rope. With everyone quiet and all eyes on him, Coach Olsen put the crescendo on the speech.

"I know you have done the work, men. You are prepared and know what to do. The only separator today between victory and defeat will be how you answer this question." And he paused the longest pause of the speech.

"ARE YOU READY TO HOLD THE ROPE?"

The team started yelling and jumping up and down in a frenzy. Feeding off the energy, they lined up and waited at the opening of the tunnel ready to take the field for the biggest game of the year.

With the eruption of the band and to the roar of the standing-room-only crowd of 80,000, the team rushed onto the field through a wall of smoke lined by the college cheerleaders. Brian always loved this part of the pregame ceremony, but was especially excited today because he knew Kelly and the girls were also in the crowd to watch. Brian waved to them from the sidelines, chuckling at seeing his girls in their little cheerleader outfits.

After warmups, the announcements, and coin toss, the kickoff officially started the contest with an explosion of the cannon that is fired every time the home team either kicks off or scores. Unfortunately for fans who love a high-scoring contest, they would not get to hear that sound too often in the first half.

Although the team's offense wasn't putting points on the board, the defense was stepping up and held the rival team's high-powered offense to just 10 points. When Brian's team went into the locker room down 10-3, they weren't depressed. As over 20-point underdogs, they realized they were actually now believers that an upset victory could be possible.

At the half, Coach Olsen addressed the team about some adjustments they would need to make in order to get back in the game. As he focused on the offensive players,

Brian and the defensive coaches gave some last-minute ideas to their players.

"Marcus, you're looking good out there," said Brian. "You've had a couple nice tackles and that one pass breakup was huge on that third and long."

"Thanks," said Marcus.

"I'm going to use you to pressure Mitchell a little more in the second half," said Brian. "You need to bring the speed to make sure he doesn't get rid of the ball in time."

"I like the sound of that," said Marcus, with a new confidence.

The second half was a similar battle like the first.

Although each team had opportunities to score, each had to settle for field goals in the third quarter. Then, after gaining some momentum on offense and adding one more field goal in the fourth quarter, Brian's team brought the score to within 13-9. With time running out in the game, the defense was still holding their own. In particular, Marcus had a number of open field tackles and had knocked down a ball as well.

His name and number was getting called regularly on the PA system and mentioned by the TV announcers who were covering the game. His mother and sister were at home watching the game with proud smiles.

After trading scoreless possessions, with only 1:36 left to play in the game and the ball on the opponent's 46-yard line, Brian's team went for a big third-down pass play. To the horror of the crowd, the pass was broken up by the opposing defensive back for an incompletion. Then Coach Olsen had no choice but to go for it on fourth down and 7. To the surprise of many fans, they tried to run the ball. Getting only 3 yards, Coach Olsen's squad had turned over the ball on downs. With 1:24 left, the fate of the team looked sealed.

Because Brian's team still had three timeouts left, they knew a defensive stop here could get the offense the ball back for one more shot to win the game. As Brian's defense took the field for what could be their last stand, he screamed, "You've been doing it all night, fellas, let's shut these guys down one more time!"

On first down, the opponents ran the ball up the middle and Marcus was in on the tackle. They only got 3 yards, but because precious time was ticking off the clock, Coach Olsen used the first of his two timeouts left with 1:20 remaining.

During the timeout, Brian had only seconds to converse with the team and send in the defense.

On second down, the opponents ran a reverse, but Marcus and the defense sniffed it out. This time they shut the running back down for no yards and Coach Olsen used their second timeout with 1:15 on the clock. This time, Brian gave his players the green light to blitz. He knew it would be a pass play and he was going to send them all. As the players turned to go back onto the field, Brian grabbed Marcus by the face mask and pulled him in close.

"Where else would you rather be right now?" he commanded.

Marcus, knowing the correct answer, grinned and said, "Nowhere, Coach!"

"Then get out there and show me something!" screamed Brian.

The players set up in their formations and Marcus and his linebackers made no secret of the fact they would be bringing the heat. As the quarterback called out his cadence, the two lines of men locked into position, ready to strike.

On the second "hut!" there was an explosion of bodies and popping of pads as the linemen crashed into one another and the receivers shot out into their routes covered closely by the defensive backs. Marcus saw an open hole and gave everything he had to get through it toward the retreating quarterback.

Just then, the offensive lineman filled that gap and locked his hands into Marcus's chest. On instinct, Marcus locked both hands around the lineman's right bicep and used them to drive his shoulder up and to Marcus's right. This off-balanced the lineman and drove him diagonally backward in the direction of the quarterback, who was looking to his left for his favorite receiver. Just as the quarterback brought the ball back to throw it, the lineman tripped and smashed into him, jarring the ball loose to a monstrous scream of the team and fans of "BALL!!!" Marcus released the lineman and never losing stride, picked up the bouncing ball and sprinted like his hair was on fire toward the end zone.

Although he was oblivious to the crowd, the roar was louder than a jet engine on the field as Marcus raced over 40 yards to put his team ahead. Even though pandemonium ensued after the explosion of the cannon, they still had to kick the extra point and hold the offense one more time for victory. Brian's team lined up for the extra point and with ice in his veins, the kicker punched it through to another deafening eruption of the crowd and another blast of the cannon to put them ahead 16-13!

But there was still 1:05 left on the clock.

Brian had one last chance to address his defense before they went out to make the stand of their lives.

"This is what you have trained for!" screamed Brian. "Since you were little kids, you have dreamed of this moment. Well, you know what? It is here, men! And now it's time to show this crowd what you're made of!"

After a squib kick, Billy Mitchell's offense started with the ball on their 35-yard line. With no timeouts remaining, the rivals were moving the ball, but running out of time. With less than 10 seconds left and their final play from Brian's team's 47-yard line, Mitchell lofted a Hail Mary pass into the end zone. Marcus and another linebacker were there to knock it to the ground, sealing the victory as time ran out and the crowd jumped the barriers and ran onto the field in celebration.

In the melee that ensued of players and coaches shaking hands among the thousands of fans storming the field for photos, somehow Brian made his way over to Marcus. Marcus gave Brian such an explosive hug that because he still had his pads on and was taller than Brian, the shoulder pads smashed Brian's lips into his own teeth, slightly cutting them. With tears in his eyes, Marcus exclaimed, "It was the move, Coach! Did you see it? I used your move!"

Not fazed by the shot in the jaw due to the adrenaline, Brian yelled over the crowd, "Did I see it? Yeah, me and 80,000 other people! They're still getting that guy's shoulder out of his earhole!" Then Brian pointed his finger into Marcus's chest and said, "That's your move now. That was all you, kid."

With the sea of people swarming all over the field, Brian tried to get to the tunnel and out of the crowd to make sure that Kelly and the girls were still safe up in the stands. Because of all the commotion, he had yet to process the team's improbable come-from-behind win.

18

Bag of Peanuts

Brian made his way back to the tunnel through all the pandemonium. Passing some of the security guards who blocked the tunnel, he was finally in a place secluded enough to be able to pull his phone out of his pocket and call his wife to make sure they were all right.

"Are you and the girls okay?" asked Brian, still breathing heavily from working his way through the crowd.

"Yes," replied Kelly. "We're fine up here. The girls had a great time and I have to admit I did, too! I forgot how much fun it was to come out to a game."

"That was some win, huh?" said Brian.

"Oh my gosh, it was incredible!" laughed Kelly. "I don't think the girls will be taking off these outfits to go to sleep tonight. They keep saying 'We won! We won!'"

"I'm so glad you got to see it and be part of it with me, Kell. This whole thing really isn't as much fun without you," said Brian.

"Thanks, hon," replied Kelly. "Now get back to the team and celebrate! We'll see you at home, and after this, I think I can say we won't miss another game."

"Okay, see you and the girls tonight ... I love you," said Brian.

"I love you, too," replied Kelly. "Oh, and one last thing ... " she paused. "I am proud of you."

After Brian ended the call, he took a moment to absorb the conversation and was just looking down at his phone with a smile on his face when he was startled by what he heard next.

"Seems like one of your best days, huh, Bri?" came a familiar hoarse voice from what seemed like out of nowhere.

Brian turned around to see the old coach standing with his arms and palms against the cool wall of the tunnel.

"Coach!" said Brian so excited to see him that he hurried over and shook his hand. "Did you see what just happened?"

"Like I said," replied the old coach, this time letting go of his grip first, "looks like it was your best day out there. It's pretty obvious the defense was the reason the team won tonight. You have a lot to be proud of, Coach."

Brian was a little bit stunned by the déjà vu of the place and conversation. Just a week earlier he remembered how things had been so different. But then something occurred to him.

"*Coach*? I think that's the first time you've ever called me that."

"Like I told you," said the old coach, "I call it like I see it. It's the first time I've called you coach because it's the first time you're finally acting like one. *Coach* is the most honorable thing a person can be called, kid. I don't take that title lightly. You may have been given the title of coach by someone higher up than you, but you earned it today because of what you did for those athletes who work below you."

"Did you see that move by Marcus?" asked Brian.

"Sure did!" replied the old coach with a smile. "Was that the move you taught him?"

"Yes," said Brian, "but using the move wasn't the only highlight tonight."

"Oh, really?" asked the old coach.

"Yes," replied Brian. "I also had a 'Holy Grail' moment tonight to go along with it!"

"Feels pretty good, huh, kid?"

"Well, let's put it this way, I'm not going to forget that one for as long as I live. But I'm also not going to sit back and quit working for another one. That moment was addictive. I'm going to continue to strive to be the best coach to have more of them."

"So, you still have the goal of being the best coach in the world?" asked the old coach.

"You bet," replied Brian. "I just wonder how I'll know if I ever make it."

"That's easy," said the old coach. "Just see what the athletes you're working with now are doing in 35 years. That's when you'll really know if you're great or not. Remember, kid, a coach's effect should last a lot longer than when a player has finished his last game."

"I'm so glad to see you, Coach," said Brian. "I put all the things you taught me to use the last couple of days and I was afraid I wasn't going to get to thank you. Meeting you has been the biggest reminder that I just love coaching. I hope you're going to be sticking around for some more lessons? The team is on kind of a roll, you know."

"I really wish I could," said the old coach, "but after tonight, I see my work is done here. I was lucky to even get a chance to come back for a little while. Now you're going to have to continue to grow as a coach and share the lessons I've taught you with others."

"I'm sorry to hear that," said Brian. "Today was one of the most amazing days I've ever been part of as a coach. I would hate for the day to end like this, knowing I might not see you again."

"There are going to be good days and bad ones too, Coach. But before I go, I think I have just enough time for one more story if you would like to hear it. This is one that forever changed my life after I heard it for the first time."

"Well, you know I love your stories, Coach," said Brian.

"Thanks for indulging your coach," said the old coach as he moved closer to Brian and started to tell his story.

"Back in the 1930s there was a couple who had been married for one year. These two people were so in love and had similar dreams of making it in show business. The girl was an actress and the boy was a playwright. They were working hard at their craft and would sit together and talk about the dreams they had of someday being the darlings of Hollywood. The girl told stories of how she would someday grace the silver screen and the boy talked about writing plays that would touch people's souls.

"But there was a big problem. At that time in America, it was the most economically depressed time in the country's history. There wasn't much need for actresses and playwrights during the Great Depression. As a result, the couple was so poor, they could barely find work. In fact, they considered themselves at that time to be lucky to have the clothes on their backs.

"Because they'd been married for one year, the man wanted to give his wife something for their anniversary. All he could afford was a brown bag of peanuts. He was embarrassed by the meagerness of the gift, but he knew he had something of more value. So when he gave her the bag of peanuts, he also gave her a note. The note read, *I wish this brown bag of peanuts was a red velvet bag of emeralds. And I promise that when our dreams come true, I am going to give those gems to you.* The girl appreciated the gift, and like many times, tough times don't last forever. America recovered, and so did the entertainment business.

"The couple worked hard and the world eventually recognized them for their incredible talent. The actress starred in many movies and won countless awards. In fact, today there are even awards named after her. And the boy went on to write plays that would change the hearts and minds of millions. Together they had aspired to their dreams, and when they attended the prestigious parties of the richest people, they were the darlings of Hollywood.

"But like tough times, great times don't last forever. The couple grew older and before their 50th anniversary, the playwright became sick. At the hospital, the couple was told his condition was terminal. Because the playwright knew he had little time left, he purchased an anniversary gift for his famous wife. When she came to see him for one of his final days, in her hand he placed a red velvet bag of emeralds. She was touched by the gift, but he knew he had something of more value. So when he handed her the bag of emeralds, he also gave her a note. The note read, *I wish this red bag of emeralds was a brown bag of peanuts. Because I would give anything to go back to when we started and do it all over again with you.*"

When he finished the story, the old coach let a tear fall from his eye. Brian, also completely touched by the story, got the point. Just at that moment, the team and coaches started pouring into the tunnel with a police escort. Everyone was yelling and jumping up and down and players pushed their way in between the old coach and Brian in the celebration. As the players were pulling at Brian to go celebrate in the locker room, the old coach pulled something from his back pocket.

"Hey, Coach," the old coach yelled from across the tunnel to get Brian's attention, "Catch!"

As he said that, the old coach simultaneously threw an object into the air over the players and toward Brian. It was thrown in a way that Brian had to reach up over his right shoulder and turn and jump to make the grab like a wide receiver. He looked into his hands and saw he had caught a brown paper bag. Realizing something was inside, Brian took a moment and looked inside the bag to see it was filled with unshelled peanuts. He smiled at the bag and then turned back to see the old coach.

BUT THEN HE WAS GONE.

Acknowledgments

No one does it alone. Every top athlete, CEO, and world leader has at least one thing in common: They all had coaches!

The goal of this book was to remind you of the importance of a coach. While I was writing it, I was constantly reminded of the coaches who taught me what to write about. Now it's my turn to point my finger and give credit where it's due. Here are eight people who have had a major impact on my coaching style and knowledge:

Bill Scarola. My first real Coach and the one who taught me lessons I am still using to this day – especially the Golden Rule.

Bill Parisi. The Entrepreneur who coached me to follow my passion and to always take big swings at the plate.

Dr. Tony Caterisano. The Professor who helped me realize when you are a coach, you first have to show you care enough to help.

Dr. Rob Gilbert. The Speaker who showed me the magic in generosity and calling someone "great" until they start to believe it.

Jeffrey Gitomer. The Author who taught me that a coach sometimes has to pull the greatness out of someone. Thanks for demanding I write this book.

Joe Kenn. The Strength Coach who exemplified being more fired up about everyone else and no matter what jersey you wear, always be pumped for your team.

Teimoc Johnston-Ono. The Olympic Judoka who proved when a coach has a passion and curiosity for something, it is the greatest way to stay forever young.

Renzo Gracie. The Warrior who challenged me to always have a smile for someone and never forget that everyone loves to be called "champ."

Whenever I was coaching, I was also lucky enough to remember to be learning. All the athletes and coaches whom I have worked alongside were coaches for me, too. Here are many of the people who taught me more than I taught them:

Chris Olsen (and all the coaches and players from Wayne Hills Football), Chris Poirier (and all the great people at Perform Better), Todd Hays, Erik Piispa, Greg O'Connor, Darren Biehler, Russ Campbell, Bill Pierce, Kristopher Wazaney, Vince Corrado, Steve Leo, Mark Williams, Brandon Wood, John Cirilo, Joe DeFranco, Sal Alosi, Dan Quinn, Jerry Palmieri, Jason Garrett, Tom Myslinski, Dave Tate, Chip Morton, Mark Uyeyama, Scott Goodale, James Jankiewicz, Harrison Bernstein, Larry Bock, Jim Naugle, Scott Altizer, Dan Payne, Brian Mackler, Alan Herman, Dave Butz, Jason Chayut, Rich Sadiv, Nick Barringer, Dan Henderson, Steve Krebs, Brian Saxton, Christian Jund, Todd Durkin, Alwyn Cosgrove, Mike Boyle, Adam Bornstein, John Berardi, Lee Burton, Gunnar Peterson, Mark Verstegen, Marc Lebert, Peter Twist, Ingrid Marcum, Thomas Plummer, Bobby Cappuccio, Maia DeRoche', Kevin Wright, Jonathan Perzley, Adam Rice, Tarek Chouja, Bedros Keuilian, Craig Ballantyne, Nate Green, Gail Cassidy, Sam Caucci, Scott Paltos, Abdallah Alawadi, Neal Wolfson, Michelle Kelly, Jeff Bregman, Josh Rupprecht, Billy Felice, Alicia Saldivar, Neal Pire, Braulio Estima, Lee Miller,

Mark Serao, Chris Vaglio, Adam Colborne, Ginger Leach, Derek Rauscher, John Gallino, Shauna Rohbock, Valerie Fleming, Greg Olsen, Kevin Olsen, Chris Long, Bobby Smith, Luke Petitgout, Rich Seubert, Gheorghe Muresan, Kirsten Kincade, Brian Toal, Justin Trattou, Jim Miller, Dan Miller, Frankie Edgar, Ricardo Almeida, Chris Simms, Matt Simms, Molly Creamer, Rolles Gracie, Roger Gracie, Kyra Gracie, Igor Gracie, Luca Atalla, Alan Teo, Sean Alvarez, Joe Sampieri, Gene Dunn, Adam Singer, Jamal Paterson, Antti Nurmi, Shintaro Higashi, Arthur Canario, Jimmy Vennitti, Barry Friedberg, Celita Schutz, Gianni Grippo, Lucas Noonan, Charlie Hoffhine, Mike Springer, Ralph Mirabelli, Andrew Tucker, Rich Venditti, John Naphor, Luis Vasquez, John Derent, Ed Tejada, Rich Thurston, Keith Gallas, Brian Roberts, Mike Parillo, J.J. Damato, Patrick Gray, Kelly Gray, Richie Mendoza, John Praino, Phil Squatrito, Keith Jeffrey, Tom Robertson, Luka Hocevar, John Annillo, Michael Soos, Johannes "Hatsolo" Hattunen, Petri Rasanen, Cory Fernandes, and Dennis Rasmussen.

Special thanks to my TFW team and global network. Now hundreds of coaches from our network we call the "Familia" help thousands of people a day around the world. Much love to all the warriors who represent the RESISTANCE and bleed the "black and gold."

I would also like to thank all the coaches past and present who I have read about. Their books are the most important part of my library and prove a book allows you always to be one degree of separation away from the greatest hearts and minds in history.

My thanks to all the folks at Wiley, especially senior editor Zachary Schisgal, who was instrumental in making this book happen. My thanks also to project editor Lynn Northrup, whose insightful comments and careful editing made the book better, and with whom I enjoyed many enthusiastic phone conversations about the project.

Tip of my hat to my greatest coaches, my parents Marty and Jeanne. Without their teachings and support, none of what I have achieved would be possible. And for the last 20 years, my parents-in-law Roger and Michelle deserve credit for doing a great job, too.

Finally, I think every coach ends up having a favorite team. I can say my favorite team is no longer the New York Yankees. It is now Team Rooney, made up of my wife Amanda and our four daughters, Sofia, Kristina, Keira, and Sasha. Thanks most of all to the "Roondogs" for putting up with a coach for a husband and father and for giving me my greatest Holy Grail coaching moments.

About the Author

Martin Rooney is an internationally recognized coach, sought-after presenter, and best-selling author. A former U.S. bobsledder, Division I track athlete, Judo black belt, record-setting powerlifter, and two-time Guinness World Record holder, Martin is now on a mission to create a world of better coaches. As founder of the global fitness organization Training for Warriors and the former COO of the Parisi Speed School, he has positively affected millions of people worldwide.

Over the last 20 years, Martin has adventured to over 35 countries and coached hundreds of athletes from the NFL, MLB, UFC, NBA, and WNBA; numerous Olympic medalists; All-Americans; and World Champions. In addition to professional athletes, he has coached hundreds of high school athletes who have gone on to compete at numerous top Division I colleges across the United States. He has also spent a decade testing the coaching principles in this book as a youth, middle school, and high school track coach.

Martin has shared his *Coach to Coach* philosophy with Fortune 500 companies such as Marriott International, Nike, Prudential, and Hasbro; military organizations such as the Army Rangers, Army Airborne, and the Navy Seals; NFL teams such as the NY Jets, Cincinnati Bengals, Carolina Panthers, and NY Giants; and universities such as Arizona State University, University of

Alabama, Oregon State University, Rutgers University, and Auburn University.

Martin lives in North Carolina with Team Rooney, composed of his wife Amanda and their four daughters, Sofia, Kristina, Keira, and Sasha.

Want to spend some time Coach to Coach?

Martin delivers high-energy keynotes and game-changing half-day or full-day coaching workshops for companies and associations around the world. For more information or to contact Martin directly, please visit www.CoachingGreatness.com or email him at Martin@CoachingGreatness.com